MORE CRICKET ON THE AIR

MORE CRICKET ON THE AIR

A further selection from BBC broadcasts

David Rayvern Allen

BBC BOOKS

Published by BBC Books
A division of BBC Enterprises Ltd
Woodlands, 80 Wood Lane
London W12 0TT

First published 1988

Details of other copyright material are on p. 190
ISBN 0 563 20649 7

Typeset in 10/12pt Times
Printed and bound in Great Britain by
Redwood Burn Limited, Trowbridge, Wiltshire

Contents

List of Illustrations

Introduction

For many people, cricket on radio means the sound of well-known voices relaying information on the current Test match. If the commentary happens to be coming from abroad, more often than not it is received by those travelling on the roads, who really should be concentrating on different sorts of line and length, or else by headphoned insomniacs whose partners might prefer them to be dreaming of fine and long legs in the land of Nod. And if the match is at 'home', in many cases the broadcasters face noisy competition from factory machinery or office typewriter.

Television claims a different hypnotic response, though coverage of the actual play and truncated highlights for news bulletins and sports summaries would be the only cognisance of the game as seen on the 'box' for the moderately interested viewer.

But cricket, of course, has successfully impinged upon other broadcasting crafts and is heard and seen in other circumstances. From the comfort of an armchair one can enjoy scripted documentary, extempore interview, head-to-head discussion, radio drama and narrated story, albeit at irregular intervals, and nearly all of those formats are to be found somewhere in this book.

The programme archive, especially where cricket is concerned, is constantly having to find room for additions. With limited space available, the decision 'to keep or not to keep' is an unenviable one for those who have to make it. Only time will tell whether the right choice has been made.

When dipping into the following pages, it is important to remember that because many broadcasts are 'off the cuff' rather than written, accustomed literary prose styles are inevitably superseded by natural conversational idioms that may appear strange at first sight. Fortunately, however, the voices of many who are part of such pieces are known to the game's devotees, and to recall their timbre when reading their comments is to gain a heightened awareness of what they have to say.

This volume, Mark Two, perhaps concentrates more on the offerings of the last twenty years than did *Cricket on the Air*, yet a mass of material still remains to be exhumed. Cricket has experienced many vicissitudes since the day in 1923 when P. B. Wilson gave the first talk on the subject over the wireless in this country, some six months after Lionel Watt had undertaken the first *commentary*, for the Australian Broadcasting Commission, on a testimonial match in Sydney. Four talks by Colonel Philip Trevor followed in 1924, and two in 1925 by a Mr Kirk and Pelham Warner, but it was not until the 1930s that the game gained regular exposure on the airwaves – helped no doubt by competition, for a time, from two French commercial stations – Radio Paris and Poste Parisien. From then on, cricket on radio

9

and, in later years, television never looked back.

If, by happy chance, a glance through this collection causes spirits to rise, particularly during those gloomy periods when the barometer falls and play is suspended, then the broadcaster's work will have been accomplished. All that remains is for me to record my appreciation of the benign assistance given by commissioning editor, Tony Kingsford, who displayed a total empathy with the project throughout; my gratitude to Julian Flanders who sought widely to unearth the illustrations, to Margaret Prythergch who foraged for material so thoroughly at the Written Archives Centre at Caversham, to my secretary, Georgina Rice-Oxley, who made enquiries and conveyed messages, and indeed to all the staff at various libraries in the BBC who put themselves out to help in so many ways. A special tap on the shoulder, too, for Richard Streeton, who kindly provided the script by Percy Fender.

Lastly, a vote of thanks to every one of the contributors who originally delivered the words within.

There are times when having a chronological mind is definitely a handicap. One stumbles across what is likely to be the earliest cricket talk on the wireless still in existence and thinks, incontrovertibly, that there is no other place to start. Well, why not? Percy Fender was always entertaining, whether chasing runs against the clock, baffling his opponents with ingenious captaincy or making sometimes controversial comments in print and on the air.

This talk was broadcast on a Saturday evening and was sandwiched – somewhat incongruously – between Mabel Constanduros and the Savoy Havana Band. In the mid-1920s 'Auntie Beeb' was starting to expand but had not yet acquired a Corporation.

Talk by Mr P. G. H. Fender
Captain Surrey C.C.

2LO, July 1925

I have been asked by the British Broadcasting Company to give you a few of my ideas on the subject of cricket. Before starting to do so I should like to make a particular point of the fact that not only is this the first occasion upon which I have had the opportunity of broadcasting, and consequently feel that it is a method which comes rather difficult to me, owing mainly to the lack of the other side of the argument, and secondly I should like to stress the fact that, although talking upon a subject which is of almost universal interest, yet I am only offering one or two of my own ideas for my hearers to discuss.

I feel very strongly – and in this I am joined by the majority of regular players and first-class cricketers – that one of the things which would tend to improve the standard of cricket in England would be a diminution of the number of first-class matches which are habitually played in sequence throughout the summer months. Putting this shortly, I feel rather that there is too much cricket: by that I mean too much strenuous competitive cricket. The consequence of this is particularly felt in a summer such as that which we are now enjoying.

I suppose the majority of regular players in county sides play with one or two breaks, each of three days, from the first week in May till the end of the second week in September. Such continuous cricket as this is apt to produce staleness and tiredness in a degree which is not good for the individual. More particularly it prevents an opportunity for the individual who may perhaps have got into one or two bad habits, to go and, by means of practice as opposed to match play, correct these faults before they have gone too far.

It is never my idea in anything to be a destructive critic, and although I do

11

not think this is the time and place to put before my hearers any scheme for dealing with this difficulty which has to be contended with by all of us, I can say that I have in the past produced and laid before the ruling bodies the basis of a scheme which would deal with this, a scheme which, if more publicity were given to it and more opportunity for its discussion provided, would in all probability prove to be a basis from which could be evolved a scheme acceptable to all counties, to the general benefit of first-class cricketers in this country.

The games recently played at the Oval and Lord's between teams representing amateurs and professionals in cricket have produced several interesting points for the benefit of those who are interested in the betterment of English cricket.

In the game at the Oval the sides were picked only from those counties who were disengaged on that date and consequently were not representative, but it may be pointed out that in the game at the Oval the professional side was more nearly the same as that which played at Lord's than the amateur side. Only six changes were made in the professional team, while it was considered that there were eight players for the amateurs who could be improved upon.

In the Oval match the Gentlemen won for the first time for a great many years, and they won by reason of two definite things which they had in their favour. Firstly because in the Oval game the amateurs were able to prevent the professionals from scoring anything but slowly between lunch and tea on the third day; and secondly because the mixture of ability, and experience of which the amateur side was composed enabled them to gauge their chances and take their risks in such judicious manner as to bring success. Against such bowling as Tate, Kennedy, Howell, Hearne, etc. the Gentlemen achieved the feat of scoring 198 runs in 105 minutes, and while a good deal of hitting had to be indulged in in order to do this, it had to be tempered with good judgement as to exactly when and how to apply the pressure.

In the Lord's match the amateur side was composed much more largely of comparatively inexperienced players: at least three of the amateur side were playing their first match in big cricket, against what might well be considered to be the backbone of English bowling. On the first afternoon when Carr and Stevens had thoroughly upset the professional bowling by their methods, these younger players were very naturally lacking in the experience which would have enabled them to continue to keep the upper hand of the professional attack. As it was, the professionals were able to recover not only their length but their morale.

The point of this, to my mind, has nothing to do with the individual batsman so much as to the fact that, had it not been necessary for the batsmen following after Carr and Stevens to, in a manner of speaking, find their sea legs, it is more than likely that more experienced players would have been able with success to have taken a few more risks and prevented the professional bowling from recovering to such an extent as to be able to terminate the amateurs' first innings for 309 runs. The weight of this was particularly felt during the second day's play, when after a comparatively slow start the professionals, with their experience and ability, were able, once on top of the bowling, to continue to keep the initiative and score 457 runs in almost the same time that the amateurs took to get their 309.

I cannot leave this subject of experience without speaking for a few moments on its twin subject, namely that of trial games for the purpose of building up an English side. In every walk of life from the very start it has been a necessary principle that there should be trials of a satisfactory description before representative sides, teams or organisations can be put in the position of standing before the world as representatives of any particular country or community. There is no earthly reason why this should not apply to cricket, and while one appreciates that the main object of the MCC in constructing a side to represent England at cricket may be mainly for the purpose of playing the game as it should be played, the vast majority of the British public (and I with them) believe that it is quite possible to construct a side which could be, at least in the opinion of a large number of people, completely representative as exponents of the game and at the same time completely representative as exponents of the way in which the game should be played. But unless a proper series of trial matches is not only instituted but carefully and properly watched and considered, not only while, meta-phorically speaking, the enemy is within our gates but also during our domestic season, such a result cannot possibly be attained by any human agency. Everybody makes mistakes at times in their judgement of players and their abilities, but a continuous series of Test trials during domestic seasons as well as while the Australians or Africans are here will help to an enormous extent those who are ultimately empowered to choose the sides, to obtain an XI to represent this country in competition with those of our Dominions whom we visit or who come here, with a much greater degree of success than that which we have been able to achieve since the war.

Nowhere can a player's ability, temperament or mentality be so well watched, gauged and properly assessed as upon the field in the course of a series of hard games. Another great point is the necessity, if a side is to produce its best, for every player to have complete confidence in its skipper, and for the skipper to have complete confidence in every member of his side. This cannot be attained unless they have played together.

To close the subject it only remains to make one further point, and that is that these trials would also assist the selectors in choosing their sides from the point of view of the adaptability of certain players to the particular conditions under which they are playing. That is to say that the selectors when choosing a side must necessarily realise and keep in their minds the fact that certain players are of such a type both as batsmen and bowlers that they are much better suited to three-day matches than to longer games, and *per contra*, certain other players are more suited to the more indefinite time such as obtains in Australia, for instance, than to the necessities and occasions which arise when a game has to be brought to a definite conclusion within three days.

In conclusion I would like to say that, with the Australians coming to visit us next summer, and the very natural and great desire which there is throughout this country to see our players at last regain the Ashes, I would very confidently suggest that, no matter what the weather conditions may be, there is the cricket ability in this country for a side to be put in the field which will not only play the game in the right spirit but also bring the next series of Test matches to a successful conclusion.

*　　　*　　　*

LEGENDARY FIGURES IN CONVERSATION

Every now and then the sightscreens from the past are gently moved aside and the listener is treated to a brief mind's-eye view from some cherished veterans. During the Edgbaston Test of 1961 against the Australians (which was drawn), Wilfred Rhodes, Frank Woolley and Sydney Barnes, two of the greatest all-rounders and one of the greatest bowlers of all time, who between them totalled not far short of 250 years, were persuaded to crank their memories.

Rhodes, Woolley and Barnes

Cricket Club, June 1961

Wilfred Rhodes: C. B. Fry always told me that the Australians couldn't play George Hirst and that they tried to hit themselves out of trouble at my expense.

George Barnwell: And that was why he said you got them out, was it?

Rhodes: That's why he said I was lucky.

Barnwell: You've had the misfortune of course to lose your sight now. Do you still manage to enjoy sitting at a cricket match?

Rhodes: Yes I do, providing there's some of my friends there, who help me to know how the game's proceeding.

Barnwell: They do say that you're a better judge of whether a batsman's played a good shot from the sound of the ball on the bat than some of the people who can actually see what's going on.

Rhodes: No, I don't think so. Unless it's perhaps hit near the splice and it just rustles a bit different – different sound.

Barnwell: But you're enjoying this match.

Rhodes: Yes, very much. I'm not enjoying the weather much, though.

Barnwell: Well, now we have Mr Frank Woolley, and you too, of course, have very happy memories of playing at a Test match on this ground, haven't you?

Frank Woolley: Yes, I have, very. And I can relate one rather funny incident that happened. That was during the first time I played here [*in 1924*]. There was a man named Parker, who was a South African playing League cricket at the time, and Herbie Taylor was short of a fast bowler so he sent for him to come in this first Test match here.

Barnwell: That was to play for South Africa.

Woolley: To play for the South Africans against England, and he bowled exceptionally well [*he took 6 for 152, but South Africa were skittled out for 30 and lost by an innings*]. I thought he was a real good bowler, but for some unknown reason when I was batting, after I've had two or three overs against him, he walked down the pitch to me and said, 'Well, Mr Woolley, do you think my field's set properly for a left-hander?' – which was a rather extraordinary thing to be asked, I thought. So I said, 'Yes, I think it seems to be just right!' He said, 'Thank you very much.'

The next over I was lucky to get three fours off him and I quite thought he would come up and say, 'Well, you've treated me pretty badly,' but he didn't, he was quite satisfied. After he'd bowled up to quarter to four from twelve o'clock, he suddenly went to the umpire and asked for his sweater and then walked straight down the pitch to me. I quite thought he was coming to say something – I walked towards him, but he just shot his head up and walked straight on and went by their wicket-keeper who walked over to him to say something, but he ignored the whole lot, walked straight into the pavilion, and Herbie Taylor who was fielding at deep mid on come running up and said, 'Frank, what did he say to you?' 'Well, nothing,' I said. 'Nothing to me – just walked on –' He said, 'That's funny. I must go and see what's wrong with him. Perhaps he's ill.' So he went into the pavilion and he found him sitting in the corner and he said, 'Well, what's wrong?' And he replied, 'I'm just tired, that's all, and I've had enough.'

Barnwell: The first sit-down strike in a Test match – the only sit-down strike in a Test match?

Woolley: The only sit-down I've seen, yes, and he didn't come out again for a long time.

Barnwell: And now here we have Mr Sydney Barnes. You, of course, were the terror of the Australians at one time. Would you have liked to bowl at them on this wicket?

Sydney Barnes: Well, I think I'd have given all that I've got, if I could have done, 'cos I would have liked to have played again.

Barnwell: Do you feel that the bowlers these days have a harder job or an easier job than you had yourself when you were bowling?

Barnes: They have a much easier job than I had.

Barnwell: Why's that?

Barnes: For instance, the first time I went to Australia [*1901–2*] there were four recognised bowlers taken – in MacLaren's team. I was supposed to be the fast bowler. There was Colin Blythe, slow left-hand, Len Braund, leg-break bowler, and Jack Gunn, slow to medium left-hand. Those were the four recognised bowlers. [*All four made their Test debuts in the first Test.*] 'Course, we had some helpers as well, but those were the recognised bowlers.

Barnwell: So you had all the hard work to do when you got out there?

Barnes: Well, there was no taking three or four fast bowlers. The second match that I played in Australia was the second Test match that I'd seen and MacLaren gave me a rest of ten minutes at the end of forty-five overs and I finished up with about seventy overs with that ten minutes rest. That's the difference between fast bowlers now and then.

Barnwell: Well, do you feel that wickets these days favour the bowlers more than they did in your day?

Barnes: Well, wickets now are slower but I should put more work into it. You can't expect a wicket nowadays – just toss the ball up and let it flip on. You've got to put the work into it to make it go. They certainly were faster in my days but, as I say, you've got to make the ball go, you've got to put some work into it.

Barnwell: And you think you could do?

Barnes: Well, I should try to . . .

*　　　*　　　*

In a conversation at his home with Gerald Nethercot, George Gunn, the individualistic Nottinghamshire and England batsman, recalled – at the age of seventy-five – some of the incidents in a striking career.

George Gunn Remembers

Midland Home Service, November 1954
Gerald Nethercot: Almost any day when there is cricket at Trent Bridge, you may notice a slightly-built man, his trilby hat tilted on one side, sitting in front of the pavilion – still watching the play as intently as he ever watched it from the dressing-room balcony, and with as keen an eye to its finer points.

George Gunn is one of those players who have become a living legend in English cricket. A man about whom stories are told wherever cricketers foregather. What a family – the Gunns of Nottinghamshire – the 'Trent Bridge battery' as they were called. George joined the Notts ground staff in 1899, following the example of his uncle, William Gunn, and his elder brother, John. All three of them played in the Nottinghamshire team together and all three of them played for England, and later George's son, G. V., became the fourth Gunn to play for Notts, and once father and son each hit a century in the same innings – which must surely be the most unusual record unrecorded by Wisden. For several seasons indeed there were three Gunns in the Notts team, and many times the Trent Bridge crowd rose to the thunder of the Gunns.

George was fifty-three when he retired from first-class cricket, having played for England fifteen times. On his fiftieth birthday he made 164 not out, and in his last Test match for England [*in 1930*], at the age of fifty-one, against the West Indies, his scores were 85 [*in an opening partnership of 173 with Andy Sandham, who went on to make 325 in an England score of 849*] and 47.

I went to see him recently at his home in Mapperley, Nottingham, to talk to him about the old days. George, looking a very spry seventy-five, was wearing his England tie and sitting in a pleasant room looking out over a rose garden. On the walls were various photographs of him on cricketing occasions. And then we started to talk . . .

I think a lot of people, very good authorities too, always maintain that you were the best player of fast bowling this country ever had. Now what were your methods?

George Gunn: Well, I used to get on the off side, and the nearer you get to the ball, well it's like being in a boxing ring. You're not so likely to get hurt. I went down the wicket, not straight in line with the leg and middle but on to the off side.

Nethercot: Who was the best fast bowler you ever saw?

Gunn: Well, Tom Wass was the best fast bowler. The best I've ever seen.

Nethercot: What was so peculiar about him?

Gunn: Well, we didn't know which way the ball was going, neither the wicket-keeper, Tommy Oates, or myself. We never knew which way it was going.

Nethercot: What about the other fast bowlers you've met. You were very friendly, weren't you, with Gregory and McDonald?

Gunn: Very fine bowlers, yes, and Gregory especially. I played against him at Nottingham in 1926 I think it was, or 1921 – I forget. But I went down the wicket to him and leaned on one or two and made them bounce back into the ring. And I said, 'They don't go far when they 'it those forms, do they?' and he said, 'No, soft as grease', and I was trying to get him going. But he took it all in good part. I thought he was a great sportsman.

Nethercot: Was that the time when you hit his first three balls to the boundary?

Gunn: That's right, yes. Bertie Oldfield was keeping wicket and he said to me, 'I don't think he'll like it if you keep hitting on, George,' and of course I agreed with him.

Nethercot: But you had a particular liking for fast bowling. Didn't you once have a battle royal with George Hirst?

Gunn: Oh yes, that was at Scarborough. I got a balloon in the first innings when Frank Field bowled me, and he was pulling my leg about bagging them in the match.

Nethercot: Getting a pair of spectacles?

Gunn: Yes. Anyway, when I went in the second knock we were on double talent money and I got well off the mark and got about 38 and I'd never walked to George Hirst, I'd never gone down the wicket to him. I thought I'd try it on George for a start because he'd been pulling my leg about going to Frank Field. Anyway when I went to George he wouldn't bowl, he simply held on to the ball and went back again. And when he came up again the second time, when he got four yards from the wicket off I went and he hung on to the ball again and went back again. Anyway the third time he came up and do you know what he did? He didn't know what to do with it. He bounced it at his own feet, and it bounced three times and I took it on the third bounce and hit it beyond cover point for four. And at the end of the match – I made 90 odd in that innings, I got out in the nineties – I went to George and I said, 'Why didn't you bowl, George, when you saw me coming?', and he said, 'Well, to tell you the truth, lad,' he said, 'I didn't know where to bowl and it upset me.' And I said to him, 'Well, if I can upset you, I can upset some of these others.' It was when he was right at the top of the bill, you see, and it convinced me that I was on a good thing and I kept it up ever after.

Nethercot: How did you learn to play fast bowling?

Gunn: Through my brother John. He was a fast bowler when we were kids. He could stand still and throw a hundred and ten yards. He could stand still on Nottingham Forest and throw off one racecourse on to the other with a stone. But when he couldn't get me out in his dinner hour – we used to play in the dinner hour – I used to tell him to throw 'em.

Nethercot: Where were you playing?

Gunn: Oh, in the passage. And he used to throw; I could trust him to throw straight.

Nethercot: But talking about McDonald, didn't you once score rather a lot of runs off him in an unorthodox fashion?

Gunn: Oh yes, at Manchester. Larwood was bowling very fast on a wicket – it was wet on top and hard underneath – and he took Charles Hallows' cap off, and Mac sat up there in their dressing-room saying what he was going to do when it was our turn. And young G.V. – he was on the reserve then.

Nethercot: That's your son, isn't it?

Gunn: Yes – and when we got off he came to me and said, 'You want to look out, Dad. When you get out there – old Mac's going to knock your blocks off – all your blocks off,' he said. So I said, 'Where is he?' 'In the dressing-room just round the corner,' he said. So I said that I would go and have a chat with him, and Whysall, my sparring partner, heard this and said, 'Do you mind if I go with you, George?' and followed me in to see Mac, and when we got there I went up to Mac and said, 'What's this you're going to do, Mac?' He said, 'You'll see when you get out there', and shook his finger – he used to point, you know, and shake his finger. And I said, 'Why, Mac, I don't think you can knock the skin off a rice pudding.' That did it. 'Anyway,' he said, 'you'll see when we get out there.'

Of course, I took first over as usual and 'Dodge', that's Whysall, said, 'If you can hit me I'll buy all our lads a big fat whisky and soda and a big fat cigar. Never mind him' – meaning me, you see. Anyway, we carried on, and I got out of the first over and when it was Whysall's turn he hit him on his left shoulder and it went for four off his shoulder, but not to hurt him, you know. He'd got to knock him out, for him to lose his bet. Anyway, to cut a long story short, I said to Mac, 'Tell you what, Mac, when we've got you where we want you I'll play you with my bat over my shoulder.' And I thought about this, and when he was giving me the long going away, on his third step from the wicket, I put my bat up over my shoulder and she flew off the end of the bat and nearly got caught at deep third man, and I was sorry I didn't bag it.

Nethercot: It hit the boundary, did it?

Gunn: Oh yes, it went to the boundary. Yes, just crept about four yards over the edge of the boundary.

Nethercot: It must have surprised McDonald quite a bit.

Gunn: Oh, he said, 'Well, I'll give in now.' That were the words he used. Good old Mac!

Nethercot: Now, what about some of your earlier recollections, George? I believe you were a big admirer of C. B. Fry, weren't you? What was the story you were telling me a little earlier about seeing him on the way to Trent Bridge?

Gunn: Oh aye, on the Trent Bridge. He was standing up in the Landau making a stroke or two on Trent Bridge as they were driving over. His wife was with him in this Landau and when I got on the ground I nipped up into the dressing-room and I said, 'He's coming.' They said, 'Who?' and I said, 'Cocky – he's got 200 on the Bridge.' Of course, Tom Wass hated the sight of him – in fact he hated all good batsmen. Anyway, when we got out there, they won the toss, C. B. Fry won the toss, and we went out and played two or three overs – perhaps three overs, I think it was – and there were some boys running wide of the screen and Tom in his run broke into a walk, because C. B. Fry had shouted down the field, 'Will you tell those boys to sit quiet.' But I'm overrunning my story. The ball before, when Tom was in his run, he drew away, you see, and shouted down the field, 'Will you tell those boys to sit quiet there.' And, of course, that nettled Tom – he went back on his mark and when he got nearly to the wicket he broke into a walk and he walked halfway up the wicket and said, 'Look here, Mr Fry, the next time you come to Nottingham, we'll have the Pavilion shifted for you.' And do you know, C.B. rolled his sleeves up to his biceps and he got 200 of the best you've ever seen. It was a fine knock.

Nethercot: Now then, George, this very famous bat of yours I've got here. I see it's inscribed 'England versus Australia, First Test, Sydney, December 13th–19th, 1907, 119–74'. Now that's a story in itself, isn't it?

Gunn: Oh yes. I went out to Australia, not with the team, but the MCC offered me a retaining fee to play in up-country matches, for £15 a match. Well, we used to get £20 in England, Gerald, as you know, for a Test match, but there was no mention of Test matches. Anyway, I'd been scoring up to this date – December the . . . what was it?

Nethercot: December 13th to 19th. You had been official scorer, had you?

Gunn: I'd been official scorer up till then yes, but the morning before the match A. O. Jones, the captain, was taken ill. He was in hospital at the time. Freddy Fane, who took over as captain, came to my bedroom and said, 'I want you to get some practice today, George. We may want you to play in this Test match,' and I said, 'Thank you, Sir.' He said, 'And if you play, I wish you luck.' Anyway, I went and got some practice and Jack Hobbs was left out of the team because he was ill through travelling, so they put me in his place. They put me in first wicket down – Freddy Fane and R. A. Young, the wicket-keeper, opened – and when there was 11 on the board a wicket fell and it was my turn – but I'm overrunning my story. After I had practised morning and afternoon, Joe Hardstaff, Wilf Rhodes and Jack Hobbs bowled to me, and then the next morning he came to my bedroom again, Mr Fane did, and he said, 'I want you to play, George – I wish you luck and I hope you get 100.' I said, 'Thank you, Sir, same to you. I hope you get one too.'

When I went down to my breakfast in the Hotel Australia there were two or three of the English boys sat together and they didn't quite agree with the selection. I heard one say to another, 'Fancy playing this fellow' – meaning me. Yes, put me on my nettle a bit. Anyway, when I walked out to bat I thought about this, and one of the gentlemen that said that, he had to come in to bat and do you know how many I put on the board while he was making 19, I think it was? Do you know how many I put on the board? I put 90 on to my score while he got 19 or 17, I forget.

Nethercot: His face must have been red!

Gunn: Anyway, it was a great day, and when I came off it was the best reception I ever had in my life.

Nethercot: So in fact you scored 100 in your first Test innings?

Gunn: Yes, and I hit twenty boundary shots in 119.

Nethercot: That's a worthwhile record anyway. You got 74, I see, from the bat – second innings.

Gunn: Second innings, yes – I missed the double. Monty Noble [*the Australian captain*] caught me out backward point off Tippy Cotter, who was a very fast bowler, and I never hit one harder in my life, I felt the bat handle tremble when I hit it. I thought it was a cert four but he bagged it. But I was a bit handicapped for the second knock, because my hands blistered in the first innings and my gloves were full of blood. The blisters broke. So of course I was a bit handicapped. But that was one of the finest catches I ever saw.

Nethercot: You must have been very proud that day anyway. How old were you then, George?

Gunn: Well, I would be twenty-six [*28 actually!*].

Nethercot: But your brother John had already played for England, hadn't he?

Gunn: Oh yes. He was a full-blown England player before I started. He had been to Australia with MacLaren. They knew of William and John, but they had never heard of George. I was a bit of a dark horse.

Nethercot: You weren't really, frankly, a strong man, were you?

Gunn: Not as a boy, no. I had rather bad health as a youngster. In fact they sent me out to New Zealand the season before that Sydney Test, and when I came back I finished top of the batting average in Nottingham, and then went out to Australia and finished top of the batting again.

Nethercot: With this same bat?

Gunn: Yes.

Nethercot: How many bats did you take with you?

Gunn: Six. Six bats and Wilfred Rhodes used this particular one. He got all his runs with that, till the last Test. I got 122 in that match and I'd seven bats in that innings. The weather was exceptional.

Nethercot: Seven bats in one innings?

Gunn: Yes. The weather was very exceptional – it was 114 in the shade, that means about 160 in the sun. And the bats had not been oiled and looked after, you know, and therefore they broke very easily. I should say that seven bats in one innings is a bit of a record too. R. A. Young kept coming out with one or two and at last he came out with an armful. The crowd kept shouting, 'Bring him another bat.'

Nethercot: Is this the match in which this broke?

Gunn: Yes, that particular bat broke. That was the first one to break – broke its back.

Nethercot: And that must have almost broken your heart.

Gunn: It did, yes. That was a real favourite – and the same with Wilf – he thought there wasn't a bat like it. It weighed two pounds eight.

Nethercot: And that's fairly heavy, isn't it?

Gunn: Very heavy, yes.

Nethercot: Going back, George, to this famous first Test innings of yours. Is the story true that you did it to music? While the band was playing you were sort of timing yourself to the music, were you?

Gunn: Oh yes. They had a military band there playing this Gilbert and Sullivan – in fact they're Gilbert and Sullivan mad in Australia – and I was enjoying it and making strokes to it, and Carter, the wicket-keeper, said to me, 'I think you're taking more notice of the band than the cricket.' And I said, 'Don't you believe it. I'm watching your fellows too.'

Nethercot: What sort of bowling did you do yourself? What kind of bowling?

Gunn: Medium pace.

Nethercot: Did you spend a long time practising the grip?

Gunn: Oh, about twenty years. I had to find it out for myself. Tom Wass, he could bowl that ball, you know, quite different to anybody else, different

23

to anybody else, different to me, my grip. But I never got it from him, he would never show anybody, old Tom. No.

Nethercot: Didn't you once give a demonstration of your grip to a certain Yorkshire bowler?

Gunn: Oh yes, Coxon. Alec Coxon. Yes, I taught him to bowl it in the bar at Trent Bridge. I said, 'I've never seen you make a ball go from leg, Alec, at this match,' and he said, 'No, I can't. I wish I could.' So I said, 'We'll fetch a cricket ball and I'll show you.' And he did. He fetched a cricket ball and we nearly knocked the doors down in the long bar at Trent Bridge. Anyway, he was so delighted when he saw it go that first time – he got that excited and he said, 'Would you come and have a go with me in the room in the morning for twenty minutes,' and I said, 'I'd be delighted, Alec.' And he finished up with 143 wickets that season. That was halfway through the season.

Nethercot: There are so many stories about you, George, that one hardly knows where to begin, but is there any truth in the one about the bowler who, seeing you come down the wicket to him, advanced towards you and shook hands?

Gunn: Yes, Cecil Parkin of Lancashire. It was at Manchester.

Nethercot: Who was the biggest hitter that you ever came across?

Gunn: Fred Barratt.

Nethercot: Of Nottinghamshire?

Gunn: Nottingham, yes. He was the biggest hitter, yes.

Nethercot: Of course, you scored pretty fast yourself from time to time, didn't you?

Gunn: Yes, I used to have fits and starts.

Nethercot: And also I think there was an occasion when you were accused of being very slow. Wasn't that against Yorkshire?

Gunn: That's right. I was batting about six hours the first innings and the Sheffield press said I never ought to play cricket again. When I went in the second time, I thought I'd just play a bit for the press, you see. The first ball I hit past cover point, a lad named Garnet Lee was my partner then. He was a very fine runner between the wickets and the best judge of a run in the country. Also the best googly bowler. Garnet Lee. He went to Derbyshire, but in that innings I just made up my mind to hit everything that came up.

Nethercot: That was the second innings?

Gunn: Yes. The second innings and there was 96 on the board and I'd got 92 of them. I finished up with 108 out of 128, something like that. That was the quickest 100 I ever got.

Nethercot: What did the press say after that?

Gunn: They didn't know what to say.

Nethercot: Tell me something about this famous birthday innings, your fiftieth birthday innings.

Gunn: Oh, at Worcester. Yes, my sparring partner, Whysall, and myself were not out, 16 and 17 apiece, overnight. When we went down to the hotel and had dinner – we'd been to a music hall after, I think – anyway, when it got to midnight we were having a drink and Whysall said to me, he said, 'George.' He just looked at the clock: it was twelve o'clock. He said, 'George, it's your birthday today. I've been out and bought some music,' and he'd been out and bought 'Watchman, What of the Night' and a selection from *Iolanthe* and some dance music, and he said, 'What about starting the concert?' So we started, and it was sunshining like billy-oh when we went to bed the next morning. Anyway, when we walked out to bat, I looked up at Dodge, and I said, 'Are you all right, Dodge?' And he said, 'Yes, are you?', and he'd only got one eye open; he'd got the other eye half shut. We managed to get going and Dodge got 70 odd and he got out, but I carried on and he helped me to get 100 on my birthday.

Nethercot: That was a good birthday present. Well, thank you very much indeed, George – you know, for talking like this. I know we could continue all night, one way and another, but I think you've said enough to remind both past and present generations what a very colourful character in the world of cricket you were. And I think, by the way, I ought to wish you many happy returns of not very long ago. How old are you now?

Gunn: Seventy-five.

Nethercot: Well, well done, you're seventy-five not out. May you get your century.

Gunn: Thank you very much!

*   *   *

One of the greatest fast bowlers of the inter-war years, Harold Larwood will for ever be inextricably linked to the notorious 'Bodyline Tour' of Australia during 1932/3. In 1983, the fiftieth anniversary of the tour, he came to the microphone in his eightieth year to tell the inside story.

Harold Larwood

Bodyline Revisited, January 1983

We found out in 1930 that he was a bit weak on the short rising ball on his leg
stump. And when I was selected to come out here, there was a meeting in
London, organised by Jardine, and they asked me if I could keep a good
length on Bradman's leg stump. They said, 'Of course, you've got to be
accurate.' They said, 'Do you think you can manage it?' I said, 'We'll have to
wait and see about that.' I was always a fast bowler. I was a little bit on the
short side, and I could get the ball to rise more than all the other fast bowlers
on the English side. How I did it I don't know, because they were all head
and shoulders taller than me, but I could get the ball to rise higher than
them. I was 5′ 8″ but I was fit; I was 11 stone 7 when I left England, and would
you believe when I got back to England I was 12 stone 7? And I never had
breakfast. I used to have a glass of beer for me lunch and a cigarette. I used
to have a good dinner at night. I always remember the drinks coming out,
and it was hot, and when the drinks came out I went up and I had a look, I
walked away. So the skipper came to me, he said, 'Harold, the drinks are
here,' he says, 'aren't you thirsty?' I say, 'Yes.' He says, 'Well, there's some
drinks there.' I said, 'No thanks.' He said, 'Well what would you like?' 'Oh,'
I said, 'a glass of beer, please.' 'Oh,' he said, 'you can't have beer out here.' I
said, 'Oh well, let's forget it.' And next time the drinks came out, right in the
centre was a glass of beer.

I used to have five close in on the leg side, just round the back. I had a
short mid off, to save the one, and I'd no slips, a short gully to save the one,
and I used to go right to the edge of the crease and bowl across the batsman. I
couldn't bowl on the off stump because I'd no men on the off side, so I had to
concentrate on the leg stump or just outside the leg stump, and I'd got to be
on the short side because, if they were pitched up, to anyone like Bradman,
naturally they'd just have found the open space on the off side. When I used
to bowl the ordinary stuff for the first two overs, I used to hold the ball
loosely for the away swinger, which in those days used to swing for two overs
or about three and then finished. And I used to have two overs with the new
ball, away swingers, and then I reversed it to leg side, where I used to go
right to the edge of the crease and I used to grip it, and it used to come back
off the pitch just a shade. I couldn't bowl an in-swinger, couldn't bowl it in
my life, but my balls used to come back a little bit – I never knew me own
pace. In England there were a lot of fast bowlers, and I never thought I was
faster than any of those. But out in Australia, especially 1932, I knew I was
fast. Because when I used to drop me left foot in England, with all me weight
behind it, it used to give a little bit on the soft grounds. But here in Australia
as I dropped my left foot it gripped, and I used to put everything into it then.

But I've never bowled as many bouncers as what these people bowl in these days. Never. And I know too that it wasn't my fault either of them. I hit Billy Woodfull in the ribs, well he wasn't a tall fella and he was crouching when he got hit, so it couldn't have been high. And poor old Bertie Oldfield got it. Well, that was his fault because he turned to hook it and missed it, and he told me afterwards, he says he never saw it after it pitched. But Lillee and Thomson, they hit people these days and there's nothing said about it. I used to get booed from start of play to finish at night, but that barracking used to inspire me.

The Fourth Test, Brisbane, 10–16 February 1933.

I'll never forget it because it was 104° about three or four days in succession, and it was the first time we hadn't got a quick wicket, and at lunchtime they were about 70 or 80 up and no wickets. So as I was walking off the ground at lunchtime, someone in the stand at the side shouted, 'When you going to get a wicket, Larwood?' So I stopped, and I said, 'What's the use?' I said. 'There's better players than these waiting to come in.' So anyway, we battled on, I hadn't got a wicket first day, and I think Australia was two hundred and something for 3, Bradman and Ponsford both not out. So I had one or two beers that night, not many but just to forget about it, see – because we never used to talk cricket at night time, we used to forget it. Anyway, next morning I shot Bradman out, I shot Ponsford out – in fact they were all out for just over the 300.

Then we went in to bat and Eddie Paynter had to go to the hospital, he was terrible. And we must have lost quick wickets. Well, I was looking to go the next in, and in walks Eddie Paynter – Jardine had sent to fetch him out of the hospital. And Eddie came out, his face was deathly white, so I said how do you feel, he says terrible. I said, 'Well, look Eddie' – fancy me telling him – I says, 'Look, Eddie, you hold the end up,' I said, 'I'll try and get a few runs.' And we got the good bowlers off and on went Stanley McCabe. And about his second ball, it was down the leg side, about a yard wide and I had a hit at it and missed it, it hit me leg, ricketed back over to the wickets. And I got out and anyway Eddie went on and he had to go back to the hospital, and then he came back next day and he finished up he got about 80, he gave us another chance to carry on and we won the Ashes.

For Larwood it had been an extraordinarily strenuous tour. He asked his captain, Douglas Jardine, if he could be rested for the final Test at Sydney. Jardine said no, so Larwood played.

We'd been bowling for about two days, I think, and as we always do when we got them all out, we went and had a shower or two and four or five of us were sitting with just a towel round us, and we'd done our batting and we'd lost one wicket [*Jardine's*]. It came to about half-past five or twenty-five minutes to six and the skipper came to the top of the little stairs, he says, 'Les, put your pads on. So and So, put your pads on. Harold, you put your pads on.'

I says, 'What me, skipper?' He says, 'Yes you, Harold.' And we heard this roar [*Sutcliffe was out for 56*] and just looked at one another, so the skipper says, 'Righto, Harold, you go in.' So I turned to Leslie Ames, I said, 'Can you get your bat ready, Les? 'Cos,' I said, 'I'm going to get out.' I was annoyed.

I went out, and the first ball I hit to Bradman at cover point. I says, 'Come on, Wally [*Hammond*].' He says, 'No, go back.' I says, 'Come on.' Well, we were both in the middle of the wicket but Donald [*Bradman*] got the ball. Now, I think he could have run up to the wicket and took the bails off. Instead of that he had a throw, and it missed the wicket, went sailing on to the boundary, made me a five with that shot. And Wally, he batted the over out and we came in.

Well, the next morning we went out, and as we were going out Wally said, 'Now look,' he said, 'just control yourself and come down to earth,' he says, 'and you'll get some runs out here today.' This Alexander from Victoria, he was fast and he was after me, I knew that, because the crowd was urging him on, so when he was bowling to me I got hold of the top of the bat. I thought, it's either you or me. I hooked him and I square cut him a few times, and Wally was the first one out [*for 101*]. Maurice Leyland came in and we got all the good bowlers off, Bill O'Reilly was off, and they put P. K. Lee on, an off-spin bowler from South Australia. I swished him to the leg boundary for four, and they still hadn't put a man there. So Maurice Leyland beckoned me down the wicket, he says, 'Have you seen the scoreboard?' I says, 'No, what's wrong with it?' He says, 'You're 98.' I said, 'Oh, that's 98 too many for me.' So I went back and the next ball, exactly the same spot, and no man on the square boundary and I was going to woof it one and I stumped me shot and old Bert Ironmonger run in and caught it with his left hand. He's never caught a catch in his life, but he caught that. The crowd, they were cheering and standing up, I had a terrific ovation. Do you know that 98, I think I'm more remembered for that than if I'd have took ten wickets if I'd have been bowling.

However, the hard Australian wickets, the springboard for Larwood's success, finally took their toll, and after bowling just ten overs in Australia's second innings he broke down.

I busted my foot and now I couldn't bowl, I couldn't finish the over [*his 11th*]. So Jardine says, 'You'll have to finish it, Harold.' I said, 'Look, skipper, I can't, it's impossible.' He said, 'Well, you'll have to.' I said, 'All right,' so I stood and just turned me arm over, against the wicket, and Billy Woodfull just pushed each ball back. Now that's where I admired him because he could have hit those balls anywhere he wanted. He just pushed them back, so I said to the skipper, 'Well, can I go off now?' 'No,' he said, 'no.' He says, 'Look, go to cover point.' Now that's the worst position in the field, to field. I says, 'Cover point?' I says, 'I can't run after them, skipper.' He said, 'Go to cover point, let somebody else run after them if they pass you.' I said, 'Righto.' And then Verity went on, and I think Bradman must have lost his head. He went down the wicket and tried to hit him, missed it, and it bowled him. And then Jardine clapped his hands and said, 'Righto, Harold, go off,' and Don and I walked off the field with one another and neither of us spoke. When I got into the pavilion, the masseur told me straightway, he said, 'You'll never bowl again without you have an operation.'

It was to be Larwood's last Test match. Eventually he emigrated to, of all places, Australia. He bore no regrets –

I'd achieved everything I wanted to achieve, because I came out of the coal mine. My ambition was to play for Notts, I got that, I played for England in England, I met the King and Queen in England, I met all the notabilities out here, Prime Ministers and raised the headlines, I mean I was entirely satisfied. Probably if I hadn't have broken down I might have just faded away.

*   *   *

Eddie Paynter had an abundance of those sterling qualities that appear to thrive on adversity. Instinctively an attacking batsman – a fine hooker and cutter – he was nevertheless a doughty defender when the occasion demanded, as well as being a fleet fieldsman with a safe pair of hands – all the more remarkable considering that the top joints of two fingers were lost in an accident when young.

Stuart Hall prompted Paynter to enlarge on the extraordinary circumstances surrounding an innings for which he will for ever be remembered.

Eddie Paynter

Sports Report, Third Network, October 1965
Stuart Hall: Eddie Paynter, the great England and Lancashire left-hand bat – the man with an average against Australia of 84.42, the highest of any England batsman. Eddie's the former bricklayer, who made history by rising from his sick-bed at Brisbane in February 1933 with a temperature of 104 to make 83 against the Australians. Well, Eddie, 22 Rupert Street, Keighley is a long way from Australia, but can you recall those moments in 1933?

Eddie Paynter: Well, I certainly can. I was ordered by the specialist to go to hospital and stayed in over the weekend. On the Monday morning I wasn't too well again and on the advice of the specialist I'd got to stay in bed and on no occasion should I go to the ground at all. Fortunately Bill Voce came and we had a wireless set in our bedroom, and as the wickets was falling, Bill said, 'What about it, Eddie?' So anyhow, I decided and I says, 'Get me dressing-gown and get a taxi and we'll go.' And as the sister saw us leave, she played 'harry' with us and said, like, it was our own responsibility if we went.

Anyhow, we went to the ground and when the skipper saw me he said, 'Well, thank you, Eddie – you'd better get your pads on and so on!' So I got my pads on, and Gubby Allen got out and I had to go straight in and that was all right for me 'cos I 'ad no waiting at all.

Anyhow, I went in and after an hour's play – the close of play on that day – I was 24 not out. Well, I went straight back to hospital and the following morning I felt a little bit better, and I went to the ground again and was fortunate to make a score of 83.

Hall: Now your [*international*] career, Eddie, was a very short one, wasn't it?

Paynter: Yes.

Hall: Only nine years long.

Paynter: Practically nine years, that's all [*1931–1939*].

Hall: What differences would you say there were between present-day cricket and cricket before the war?

Paynter: Well, in my opinion in present-day cricket the batting is letting us down, more than anything. I don't think they're batting the ball as it should be 'it. I mean, there's 'alf-volley after 'alf-volley and also bowls that I'm sure can be 'it into the outfield with a mid on and mid off 'alfway back. You don't see it, but I think it should be 'it out there with batsmen using their feet. I don't think they use their feet like they did in the olden days.

I mean, I can remember both Ernest Tyldesley and myself against Kent at Old Trafford and we both got 'undred apiece, and Tich Freeman came on to bowl and I 'it 'im for four fours in one over. I got in trouble through it. But bear in mind I got a ton. Ernest Tyldesley came down the wicket to me, he says, 'Eddie, don't do that.' I says, 'Do what?' I was real perked because I got a hundred and 'it for four fours. He says, ''It 'im for two in one over, Eddie.' He says, 'If you keep 'itting 'im for four they'll take 'im off and we want 'im on.'

On a later occasion Eddie Paynter was asked if the most exciting matches for him, apart from Tests, were the Roses games.

January 1972
Paynter: Definitely. It was worse than playing in a Test. Was in our day. I don't know what it's like now. I don't watch much cricket these days.

30

I should think the Roses matches in our day were keener than what it was in England side. It's a lot to say but I think it were true. They used to kid us in the dressing-room, we used to kid them, and then when we got on the field all 'ell was let loose.

*　　*　　*

THE 'ROSES' MATCHES

Whether quite the same intensity in the 'Roses' encounters as described by Eddie Paynter exists nowadays is debatable. Certainly nobody was more qualified to give a balanced view of the matches than Cecil Parkin, who had played for both counties. Parkin, dubbed 'cricket's comedian' because of his unquenchable humour, had made a single appearance for Yorkshire before it was discovered that he had been born some twenty yards the wrong side of the county boundary. If only his mother had known she was delivering from the wrong end! Subsequently, he turned out for Lancashire and England.

In Britain Now
Cecil Parkin

August 1940

August bank holiday. How many Lancastrians and Yorkists must have spent it watching the two battles of the Roses at Old Trafford or Headingley. This year they're away on other business, but perhaps, like myself, they will be thinking of some of the tense moments in those games.

I remember our first game against Yorkshire at Old Trafford in 1919 after the last war. In the first innings I hit David Denton on the thumb causing him to retire in great pain. He didn't expect to take part again in the game, but in Yorkshire's second innings we were striving hard to get them out. I can fairly see David now in the dressing-room, changing to come in to bat last. He'd not time to take his collar and tie off before he was required to take his place at the wicket to try and save the game for Yorkshire with only five minutes to go. I was bowling at the time and the crowd was at fever pitch. About the third ball I knocked David's wicket out of the ground, thus gaining for ourselves a great victory. I shall never forget the scenes. The crowd surged on the ground and my poor back was red raw with the spectators' congratulations. On our arrival at the pavilion David was still stuck at the pitch *wondering* how he was out.

On another occasion at Old Trafford – I think it would be about 1925 – the last two Yorkshire batsmen were in. Wilfred Rhodes and Rockley Wilson wanted three runs to win. You can understand the excitement to a crowd of over 40,000. It finished a drawn game, but perhaps Yorkshire were afraid to have a go for those last three runs. The match at Headingley in 1924 will live in the minds of both counties for years. On the last day Yorkshire wanted 58 runs to win. Most of our Lancashire supporters had returned home, evidently not liking to see our defeat. Dick Tyldesley and myself were the opening bowlers and I got Sutcliffe out first over – a great batsman to get rid of. I said to Dick, 'We'll lick 'em, stick at 'em' – and we did. Poor old Dick bowled like a hero and everyone of our players fielded like cats, and we won a really great victory, putting Yorkshire out for 33. Our captain, poor old Jack Sharp, simply went mad with joy and I believe there was no more business done in Manchester that day.

I like the way the Yorkshire side is skippered. For instance, last year at Old Trafford I was on duty coaching. About ten in the morning I went into Brian Sellars, the Yorkshire skipper's, dressing-room and found he was already changed with his pads on. I was amazed at his early arrival, and he told me Leyland had a bad leg and he was going to the nets with him to see if he was fit to play. That showed great keenness. Yorkshire won that match, Bill Bowes bowling splendidly. I shall never forget the Yorkshire skipper going to their players' room. He just shouted, 'Well played, lads! Well bowled, Bill. Don't get swollen-headed, you play Warwickshire tomorrow.'

It's a delight to me on these matches to walk round the ground and hear the remarks and arguments. It's better than going to any theatre. I remember one of the Lancashire players getting bowled out for a duck and, as he was taking his pads off, in walked a terrier dog. The player in question threw his pads at it and told it to get out. 'Do you know whose dog it is?' asked one of the other players. 'No,' he answered. 'Well – it's the captain's dog, Spot.' Up he jumped and ran to the door, shouting 'Spot! Come on, Spot, good dog!' It makes a difference being a captain's dog.

*   *   *

Five years after hostilities round most of the world had ceased, two rather unlikely fellows were solicited for their opinions on the traditional rather more domestic joust that was life and death to many of the sporting residents at either end of the Pennines. Having just watched Lancashire beat Yorkshire by 14 runs over Whit weekend, the two Fellows, of St John's College, Cambridge, by the way, and eminent mathematicians and astronomers alike, came together for a 'head to head' at the microphone.

The Wars of Lancaster and York

Third Programme, June 1950
Fred Hoyle: Now, Lyttleton, you're an impartial outsider in these wars of

York and Lancaster, and no doubt you'd see the match differently from a Yorkshireman like myself. What did you think of it all?

R. A. Lyttleton: Well, I've seen Lancashire and Yorkshire separately playing other sides on many occasions, but this was the first time I had seen them together. Of course, I'd also heard long ago that anyone wanting brighter cricket need not look to these Roses matches for it. But apart from the efforts of one or two of the players this particular match, I think you will agree, was by no means of the usual grim pattern.

Hoyle: Well, it certainly would have been if Yardley hadn't taken a risk by declaring on the third morning even though the Yorkshire total was still more than 60 runs behind Lancashire.

Lyttleton: Yes, and credit is also due to Howard for being determined to take up the challenge. Do you realise this is the first of these Lancashire versus Yorkshire matches that has been finished since the war? Lancashire could easily have played safe, but instead of that they went for the runs, and their 117 was a lot less than they might otherwise have made in their second innings. Yorkshire were certainly given the time to get the 182 they wanted, you know.

Hoyle: That was so. One of the best things was that after the uneventful play of the first two days such a tense struggle should have come about on the last day, played amid the sort of scene that showed you that not all Yorkshire grit is metaphorical.

Lyttleton: I don't think it is, and I don't think I remember an innings of more varied incident and changing fortune than Yorkshire's final attempt to win on that very awkward wicket. I thought one of the highlights was Close's brief innings. Had he stayed only a few minutes longer Yorkshire must have won easily. I feel pretty sure also that he did a unique thing in these matches in hitting a six off his very first ball, and what a tremendous six it was too! If some of the bygone Yorkshire stalwarts were alive today they would have turned in their graves at this unusual piece of levity on such a serious occasion!

Hoyle: What impressed me about that, this fourth innings, was Hutton's attempt to command the situation. At first Yorkshire played the bowling strictly on its merit, but when this produced only about 40 runs in nearly an hour and a half and a tame draw seemed nearly certain, Hutton quite evidently made up his mind to take every reasonable risk to put Yorkshire ahead of the clock. And within twenty minutes he'd not only done that but he'd put the side in a position to win. You know, I can't help feeling that in these critical situations there's a strong analogy between cricket and scientific research. The same qualities are needed in both. Mere caution is practically useless. Enterprise is also needed, but not just unrestrained enterprise. What you need is a judicious mixture of the two, and the skill at any stage lies in getting the right mixture.

Lyttleton: Well, at any rate in cricket it's well known that on a doubtful wicket one can play too carefully. But your analogy fails, I think, in one respect. In cricket a mistake may be fatal and lose the match, as we saw on Tuesday. But in science a few mistakes hardly matter so long as you get to the right result in the long run. A lot of great advances, you know, have come from ideas that were not themselves correct.

Hoyle: But don't let's be too philosophical. Let's get back to the match. Not all the good things were confined to that fourth innings.

Lyttleton: No indeed. Some of the bowling, especially by Lancashire, was exceptionally accurate even for first-class cricket. I was particularly interested in watching their new man, Berry. He seemed to me to have the great quality of spinning the ball forward toward the slips, as it were. This kind of overspin not only helps in flighting the ball, but also makes it very lively off the wicket. It's by no means at all known that this is the real secret of spin. Of course the Sheffield wicket suited left-hand bowling, but my guess is that Berry could turn it on almost any wicket.

Hoyle: But you have got to remember on both sides the bowlers owed a lot to the high standard of fielding. I think nearly everyone shone at one time or other, but Grieves, the Australian, stood out all the time. His quickness near the wicket put me in mind of Keith Miller. I personally don't think it entirely an accident that the one Australian who chanced to be playing should have distinguished himself in this way. In English cricket not half enough attention is paid to the importance of fielding.

Lyttleton: You're a believer in the value of fielding, then?

Hoyle: I certainly am. I firmly believe that a sufficiently good fielder can be worth his place without a doubt. I should say this applied even in Test cricket. In my view the Australians realise it, and this is one of the reasons their bowling always seems so strong, no matter how good the wicket they're playing on. Every chance is snapped up, or nearly so, and also a good deal that we mightn't even regard as chancish.

Lyttleton: But would you recommend a team composed solely of eleven fielders?

Hoyle: Well, of course that alone might lead to awkward consequences, but it's along the right lines. I think there is such a thing as hostile fielding, just as much as there's hostile bowling and batting, and that it's just as important.

Lyttleton: And I suppose you think the captain should be the one that sets the example?

35

Hoyle: Very much so, if he can. We had an excellent instance of all this with the Cambridge University side of last year under Insole. At the start of the season they were very weak, while Oxford were very strong. But by the time July arrived Cambridge were able to give Oxford a good trouncing against all the odds. I attribute this very largely to the captain, Insole, whose personal example of aggressive fielding gradually had its effect on every department in the Cambridge side, and transformed it into a good one.

Lyttleton: At Sheffield, of course, it was a slow bowler's wicket, and Lancashire realised this to such an extent that we hardly saw anything of their pace bowlers. One over between them was all they had in that final innings. Imagine that! Other bowlers actually rubbed the ball in the dirt to get the shine off, instead of the usual practice of trying to keep it on. But then they'd seen Trueman of Yorkshire trying to get some pace out of the wicket earlier on. By the way, I hope that the next time I see this young fast bowler's action – you know, he seems capable of being pretty quick, but he's rather inaccurate as yet, I thought.

Hoyle: Trueman's fast all right, but how do you think he compares with the great fast bowlers of times gone by? I mean such men as Richardson and Kortright, who are often said to have been even faster than Larwood.

Lyttleton: Well, if reports are correct they must have been terrifyingly fast, but I fancy there's some tendency to a little affectionate exaggeration where these old players are concerned. It all seems to me a pity that the speed of fast bowlers is not accurately measured, placed on record, just as is done for sprinters and cyclists and such like. The prestige of being high in such a list, you know, might do far more to encourage fast bowling than all the heart-breaking talk about the giants in the past that we hear.

Hoyle: What sort of speeds of the ball d'you think such measurements would reveal?

Lyttleton: Well, it's difficult to say with any certainty. But I should think speeds greater than seventy miles an hour, or about a hundred feet a second, would be found rather rare. This is only a rough estimate, of course. That's why I should like to have some of these measurements. But come what may, I believe that speeds twice this amount could be quite unknown.

Hoyle Is that really so? I'm sure very few cricketers have any idea of these points. Why, only the other day I came across a statement by a most distinguished cricketer to the effect that Kortright bowled at 2000 feet a second, and his contemporary Cotter at 1950 feet per second. These are about twenty times your estimates.

Lyttleton: Well, of course I never saw either of those gentlemen bowl, but if they really had anything like that speed then we can be quite sure the age of great fast bowlers is past and gone for ever. And a good thing too, I should say, for the personal safety of ordinary mortal batsmen. Can you imagine what 2000 feet a second would be like?

Hoyle: I can form a mild idea, anyway. I should think that at that speed the ball would emit a horrific whistling sound and would go clean through any bat, not to mention the unfortunate batsman and wicket-keeper. And it's even doubtful that the pavilion at Lord's itself would entirely arrest its career. This, I think, would greatly astonish the members, not least those who think the age of fast bowling to be past. Just think of the poor batsman's relief in getting away from Kortright, and only having to face Cotter with his mere 1950 feet a second at the other end. [*2000 feet per second is over 1350 miles per hour.*]

Lyttleton: It reminds me of the famous incident related by Jenner. He was the first Cambridge captain, you know, back in 1827. Apparently he used to tell a tale of a very fast ball he once saw that broke the bat, then the batsman's leg, then hit both the middle and leg stumps, and after passing through a coat held by long stop, it killed a dog before finally disappearing through a stout oak paling at the far end of the ground. I should think a return to this sort of thing would satisfy even the warmest clamourers for brighter cricket.

Hoyle: But we could hardly expect brighter cricket than this particularly Lancashire and Yorkshire match.

Lyttleton: I think this question of brighter cricket is more a subjective matter than an objective one. To some people it simply means fast scoring. For them, I suppose, the ideal state of affairs would be for the bowling to consist entirely of long hops and full tosses down the leg side, and bowled to an offside field. In this way a scoring rate of several hundred an hour could easily be arranged. But I'm afraid this wouldn't suit me, and I fancy its advocates would soon tire of it.

Hoyle: But it would please the cricket statisticians, although I think these are the very last people whose wishes should be considered. I'd like to see batting averages done away with altogether.

Lyttleton: I quite agree. So would I. But of course everything under the sun has been suggested from time to time for producing brighter cricket.

Hoyle: Yes, there'd be no difficulty, I suppose, in drawing up a long list – smaller bats and balls, larger stumps, smaller grounds, time limits, changing the lbw rule, abolishing the championship, almost anything you like.

Lyttleton: There's always been a lot of that sort of thing. The literature of cricket shows it very clearly. I possess some authoritative volumes on cricket of about fifty years ago. They were published at the beginning of this century. Chapter after chapter deplores such things as the prevalent colossal scores, the excessive pad-play by the leading batsmen, how certain strokes, such as the cut and the glide, are disappearing from the game, the lack of really fast bowlers, the general decadence of the game as a whole. And according to these critics all this was supposed to be happening in the days of C. B. Fry, Ranjitsinhji, Victor Trumper, Grace, and so on, not to mention the demon fast bowlers. I understand the same discontent can be traced back to well before the 1860s.

Hoyle: Well, no doubt it goes back as far as cricket itself, which I understand from Dr Charlesworth, the ancient historian, had its origins in the ritual practices of early Egypt about 3000 years before. But coming back for a moment to this question of a speed of 2000 feet a second, I've just been doing a little calculation, and I find that a ball bounding from the Lord's pitch with this speed might end up as far north as the Mill Hill observatory, where no doubt it will be mistaken for a meteorite.

Lyttleton: There was a time when scientists refused to believe in meteorites, but it couldn't have been during the age of great fast bowling, could it? This, you know, raises an interesting astronomical question. How do you think, Hoyle, a celestial visitor from another planet might report back on our game of cricket? He would certainly regard it as one of the strangest, if not *the* strangest, of all human activities. Suppose you were invited to write such a report. How do you think it would run?

Hoyle: All right. I'll have a shot at it. Let's start something like this: The first interplanetary report defined cricket as a curious activity of several nations of the planet Earth. It goes on to say: Large numbers of what we may term 'monkeys' actually pay good money to attend matches of the cricket. Those monkeys are termed the 'crowd'. They group themselves in close-packed array around a circular plot of grass. On this plot other monkeys dressed in white perform truly weird and wonderful convolutions. These performing monkeys stand on their hind paws, and two of them, termed the 'strikers', grasp ingeniously-shaped pieces of wood in their front paws. Apart from these wood-holding monkeys there are eleven others on the plot grouped around in hostile attitudes. One of these latter hurls a hard red sphere towards one of the wood-holding monkeys whose duty it appears to be to strike it with the utmost violence. It must be admitted that both in propelling and striking the sphere, the creatures in some nations have attained to a quite astonishing degree of skill. Then, I suppose, it might go on something like this: A special endeavour of the wood-holding monkeys is to strike the sphere off the enclosed plot altogether. Any such occurrence is greeted with a hideous demonstration from the crowd-monkeys who beat their front paws together in a transport of rapturous ecstasy. Should a wood-holding monkey so misjudge the trajectory of the sphere that it strikes certain stakes driven into the ground, and known as 'wickets', the beating of front paws may sometimes rise to a deafening intensity.

Lyttleton: Yes, that's pretty good. But what about all the clapping for the centuries that we have?

Hoyle: Right, right, right. But more amazing still is the beating of paws associated with certain quotas of runs. These particular quotas, strange to say, bear not the smallest relation to the game itself, but are based on the curious fact that the Earth-monkeys, for some unknown reason, count in the scale of ten. For example, if a wood-holding monkey should strike a number of runs equal to the square of ten, an ungovernable orgy of paw-beating breaks out immediately in the crowd, but astonishingly when the runs reach the square of seven or eight or such like, it is received in utter silence. Why this should be so we've been entirely unable to discover, but such irrational actions form an important part of the appeal of cricket to the Earth-monkeys.

Lyttleton: Yes, it just shows how absurd things become when the element of human emotion is omitted. But I'm afraid the Sheffield crowd had no opportunity to show their appreciation of any individual batsman reaching the square often. But they were just as generous, I thought, in their applause when several reached exactly half this number. By the way, there seemed to me to be more accommodation for spectators at the Bramall Lane ground than on any other cricket ground I've been on.

Hoyle: And I should think the largest crowd was present on the last afternoon when the news must have spread round that a close finish would take place. Even the bleachers were pretty full then.

Lyttleton: Yes, and it all added to the general excitement. Things were not quite as bad as the historic 1882 Test match at the Oval. Australia won then by seven runs, and according to one commentator men noted for their coolness at critical moments trembled like a leaf. Some were shivering with cold, and some even fainted. At times there was an awful silence. But, of course, we didn't get much beyond the awful silence stage at Sheffield. But amidst it all I thought the calmest man in the ground was Hutton himself, on whom so much depended. I never quite realised till that last afternoon the extent to which he is the pride of Yorkshire. They've certainly taken him to their hearts. I am sure he overjoyed his admirers even though he didn't quite manage to pull off the match. I feel certain not a single one of them could have been disappointed with him that afternoon.

Hoyle: Well, I don't know about that. There was a Yorkshireman near me I must tell you about. He came to the ground without his glasses. He only discovered this when the players came out after lunch. I heard him say to his friend, 'Eh, lad, I shan't see a ball without my glasses. I shall have to go home and fetch 'em.'

Lyttleton: Yes, I did notice someone leave next to you almost as soon as the play started. But I thought he came back an hour or so later.

Hoyle: He did, and he was looking even more upset than before, so much so that his friend said, 'What's t'matter, lad?' To this he replied, 'Eh, I've had an awful shock. When I got home I found my wife embracing t'postman.' To this his friend said, 'Oh aye now, let me tell thee something. Tha's got another shock coming. Len Hutton's out.'

* * *

Bill Bowes, who died in 1987, was one of the most intelligent fast-medium bowlers that ever played for Yorkshire. After his retirement from the game he developed into a fluent writer and broadcaster, and his reminiscences complete what is, in effect, a ten-year cyclical look at the tribal confrontations.

Memories of the Roses Match
Bill Bowes

Home Service, August 1960

This fixture, now being played at Old Trafford, is the 170th Roses match – a traditional game of *cricket* between Lancashire and Yorkshire which is played every Bank Holiday, Whitsuntide and August, alternating in the two counties, and first played 111 years ago. It is, without question, one of the main sporting events in the North of England, and irrespective of the 'gate takings' or the size of the crowd on the ground, there is hardly a man in the North of England who will not turn on his wireless set, nip out for a paper, or ask his friend 'How's t'match going?'

I don't know that it is a fixture which interests the rest of England. I don't know that the Lancastrian or the Yorkshireman wants it to do so. It is the sort of thing they like to keep for themselves, a throwback to the times when the House of Lancaster and the House of York were at 'swords drawn'. It's a personal scrap, a serious business between opponents who each admire the ability and fighting qualities in the other, each out to thwart the other; and so far as the watching public are concerned, an occasion when national pride momentarily takes second place.

The Old Trafford Test match takes place in July just before the Roses game. I remember Len Hutton playing in a Test match at Old Trafford and with a century behind him he was beginning to show some lovely shots. There came the plaintive shout of a Yorkshireman in the crowd, 'That's enough now, Len. Save a few for Roses game next week.' Spectators for yards around grinned, and one shouted back, 'Nay, tell him to gerrum while t'goings good, he'll noan get chance next week.'

From a player's point of view, a good performance in the Roses game is the best guarantee for consideration by the England selectors. The selectors are not expected to know anything about the deep feelings of County pride and determination which are stirred by these Roses games, but they do know that every run has to be fought for, maximum effort goes into every detail of batting, bowling and fielding. The qualities needed to do well in the Lancashire and Yorkshire game are the same as those needed in Test matches. Cyril Washbrook, who has scored more runs for Lancashire against Yorkshire than any other player, says, 'The Roses game is the next best game of cricket to an England–Australia Test match.' Sir Len Hutton is on the side of the majority who claim the Roses match is the best game of cricket in the world, but adds rather pawkily, 'No matter what you do in a Lancashire–Yorkshire game, whether you score a duck or a century you always please a lot of people. The crowds are always nicely balanced, but in a Test match a "duck" pleases or disappoints everybody depending on whether you are playing in Australia or England . . . if you know what I mean.' Former Australian fast bowler Ted McDonald who later played for Lancashire said, 'These games with Yorkshire are the best of the lot.' Present-day Australian cricketer with Lancashire, Ken Grieves, says, 'I cannot imagine a game better to play in.'

It is strange then that this enjoyment cannot be treated in terms of chuckle and humour. It is mostly a relish for the discomfiture of the opposition. Maurice Leyland, former Yorkshire left-hand batsman, who can tell a funny story about most cricketers, sums it up best. 'We played these games too earnestly, too seriously for humour, but I once remember playing an innings at Old Trafford, stonewalling for four and a half hours to save the game for Yorkshire. Long before I'd finished the barrackers had now't else they could say, and when I was going through t' pavilion at close of play, a great friend of mine, a Lancashireman, stopped in front of me and said, "Maurice, you . . . you . . . you . . ." He couldn't think of anything bad enough and he just turned on his heel and went.'

I asked Arthur Mitchell if he could remember anything funny happening in a Roses match. 'Aye,' he said, 'I remember Percy Holmes at second slip appealing for an lbw. He wor t'only man to appeal, and t'umpire gave Charlie Hallows out. That wor funny!' When I put this question to Brian Statham he replied, 'I remember once when Yorkshire had us on the run, Ken Grieves scored 70 and saved the game for us. He was dropped seven times – five times in three overs just after he went in. I never saw Yorkshire faces so glum, I did laugh.'

My own funniest memory is of Jack Iddon batting at Bradford. Maurice Leyland, fielding at third man, had thrown his arm out a few weeks previously. He couldn't throw the ball back, he just had to lob it underarm. Iddon noticed this, but what he didn't know was that Maurice could raise one throw in ten weeks. Ten weeks – that was the recovery period, and Leyland daren't waste that one throw. Iddon's runs got cheekier and more daring, until finally he shouted to his partner, 'Run two, he can't throw.' Leyland's little legs sped to the ball, he picked up and let go his one throw. Iddon was run out by yards, indeed he didn't complete the run. He stopped in mid-wicket, wagged his fingers at Leyland, and said, 'Maurice, you . . . you Tyke! Kidding me. I oughter known not to trust a so-and-so Yorkshireman.'

Perhaps the loveliest story is told by Norman Kilner – a brother of Roy Kilner – who was staking a place in the Yorkshire side just after the first world war. In a lovely broad accent it goes something like this. 'I wor batting at Sheffield at t'end furthest from t'pavilion. Mr Wilson, Yorkshire captain, was my partner, and I cut a ball from Dick Tyldesley square towards Grinders stand and I shouted to Mr Wilson, "Come two". I scampered up pitch, turned and went off to t'other end wi' my head down, and theer wor Mr Wilson, resting on his bat and watching fielder pick t'ball up. "Norman, old boy, I'm frightfully sorry," he says.

'By this time ball wor half way back to Dick Tyldesley. I lost my bat turning round to go back, so I gave it up, picked up my bat, but as I did so I noticed Dick Tyldesley reaching for the ball knocked one o't bails off with his arm but almost in't same movement he knocked t'other bail off wi't'ball. I walked slowly back up t'pitch, but when I got five yards from home I did a full-length dive into my crease and said to t'umpire, "I'm not out, amn't I, Jack? He broke wickets wi' his arm." Jack says, "He did an all, lad. Not out." Dick Tyldesley looked at me, and what he didn't call me.'

Norman, as he told the story, leaned back in his chair and laughed in lively recollection. 'Ee, they were grand days,' he said.

They were, too. To have shared in a Roses game either as player or spectator is an experience which appeals to the northerner. No quarter is given or asked. It is a needle game and the humour lies in the needle pricks. Of those 170 games played, Yorkshire have won fifty-eight, Lancashire thirty-nine. The chuckles, so to speak, have gone both ways, and at Leeds last Whitsuntide Lancashire had the biggest laugh of years. On a Yorkshire pitch they gave Yorkshire a licking in two days.

*   *   *

CLUB COLLOQUY

The Concise Oxford Dictionary *definition of 'club' is an association of persons united by some common interest, meeting periodically for shared activity or socially. As far as we are concerned, all that means is that cricket clubs are no different from nearly all the others, in that they provide regular opportunities to sink a few pints and have a darn good 'natter'. Cricket is the catalyst, of course, and is naturally important. Well, of course it is. Of course . . .*

Sometimes the bonds are haphazard and very occasional and often the people diametrically different. But whether the surroundings are complemented by parked Porsches beside the village pub or empty beer crates beside an outback filling station, the sound of wood on leather lures men from their everyday occupations and makes them want to tell the tale.

Cricket at the Spout

BBC 2, December 1974

Bill Ainsley: The Spout House was the local gathering point to get to know t'news. It goes back to 1550 at least, and of course there's always been t'cricket team for over a hundred year attached to this place, like grown familiar. We're all playing cricketers; me grandad, like, he was secretary for 72 year, and he died in 1950, so that must have been from 1878, and I took over when me grandad died, like. Me grandad lived for his cricket, an' all, like.

David Bean: Bill Ainsley, publican, farmer and cricket secretary, can trace his ancestry back nearly 500 years. There was always an Ainsley at Spout House, or the Sun Inn, Bilsdale, North Yorkshire, as the new licence calls it, and always as far back as anyone knows a Bill Ainsley in charge. William Edward was the father of today's William George.

Bill Ainsley: Me dad was a cricketer – a fast bowler, I think he hung up quite a few people about in his time. He was a good bat, and all, and keep. Aw, you couldn't play good enough for him.

David Bean: Bill's grandfather – cricket secretary for seventy-two of his eighty-seven years – was plain William.

Bill Ainsley: Me grandad, like . . . even when we were only very little he was learning us to play cricket. He used to go to Scarborough every Festival, and as soon as we were big enough to take an interest, he used to take us.

David Bean: Latest in the Bill Ainsley line is William Martin George, aged eleven, and still learning cricket, helped by Uncle Basil – Spout's wicket-keeper from the farm next door. Then there's an Uncle Jim who captained the team in the thirties – he's moved out of Bilsdale now. Then there's an Uncle John, who lives in retirement a mile or so away from the Spout. Aged seventy-seven, he remembers the team at the century's turn.

John Ainsley: Ah don't know, t'cricket . . . they give their heart an' soul to cricket, and not only in a match same as last night, but every night in cricket season. The cricket ground used to be . . . anywhere up to twenty or thirty practising. Well, in my time it got that bad, you were very lucky if you got hold of a bat. So me father said, well, he said, this job's no good, he said, you comes from long into Bilsdale can't have a bat, he says, we'll make it ten minutes. And he was there on the ground with his watch . . . he let the others bat for ten minutes. When we were practising on the night, he would come up and the first thing he did, he would get hold of the three stumps and he throwed them to a side. Now then, he said, here's a match box, four and a half yards, hit that.

David Bean: Spout House cricket team plays in the local Faversham League, two or three evening matches a week during the short summer, amongst the livestock, on a sloping field whose wicket seems almost carved out of the rough pasture. Above it presides a memorial stone to Grandfather William Ainsley, and even he may not have been born early enough to remember the wicket's origins.

Bill Ainsley: Away back sometime last century this patch been levelled. It would have been done with spades an' shovels an' picks an' all, and then when they got it levelled, they went up into t'wood – right up into t'top of wood yonder – and they cut the roller out of a big rock and brought it down a rope – I think they had a lot of men and ropes an' props an' borrows an' one thing an' another, which must have been a terrible job getting it down that 'illside. Boundaries to this field is four in the field and four if you're lucky enough to hit clothes posts there. Occasionally cows or sheeps got hit. Me Uncle John remembers me pa hitting it over that tree there, but seems as though folks don't hit 'em quite so far now, I think, as they used to do.

David Bean: The heroes of the Spout House are recognisable to today's players because they were fathers, grandfathers, uncles, cousins – mostly, like today, small farmers themselves, with a leavening of mighty blacksmiths and hefty millers. The same names carry through: Ainsley, Garbett, Wood, Waid, Noble, Allison. None of them played for England, or even Yorkshire, although one – John Wood – once bowled Dr W. G. Grace and became a hero for ever in the eyes of Bilsdale. But in this great county of cricket they played in the way that made Yorkshire cricket famous, they played hard as if the game was life itself.

One man who became something of a local legend in his own lifetime was gamekeeper John Willie Noble, all-rounder from the thirties. He can still remember like yesterday a match played before the war at Carlton – a village up the other end of the Dale.

John Noble: I was put on to bowl that day – and I took seven wickets for five runs. That was the winning of that ball, it was given, I don't know who gave it, but it was put into me hands. Can't tell you the history of the ball, but it went into my hands, and it's still stayed with us for the rest of my life. And this is the bat I won in the Faversham League. And I think the one best game that ever I had with this bat was a team that was picked to go down to Firth College – to play against the Beagle team – the college team. We got out there, and I got to know'st who I was playing up against – Hampshire fast bowler. Put shivers up me, first ball; just went past like a flash of wind. I got on top of him; I was driving him right through the afternoon, right back over his head; and I managed to make fifty before he did actually shift my pegs.

John Ainsley: We were playing cricket on t'fair ground's cricket ground. I believe it was Amsley we were playing – I don't go back. And, day before, this shower came down – we had the policeman – the policeman come down from Chuckgate on his pushbike to tell me ye had to keep off the road as there was a charabanc coming up. Road wasn't as it is today and it was all ruts, you know, and we were playing cricket that afternoon of the charabanc, we could see it coming up with the white dust up the road – it was lifting it up. And we knocked off playing cricket, and we all went to the wall agin' the road, to see it pass. And then I saw the first motor-car come down Bilsdale – and it was, I don't know what year that was – I would only be about five years old – I saw the first motor-bike come down – and I saw the first aeroplane fly o'er, so I didn't do too bad.

David Bean: The Allison family, Bilsdale for generations, still raises stock on the valley side, and young Jules Allison is captain of the Spout House XI.

Jules Allison: I really started by playing with Brian Ward and Kenny Ward, and we used to play out on a bit of strip there. Kenny used to take the Australian team, Bill Lawry, Simpson, Neil Harvey and all them, and Brian and me would take the England team, which was probably Geoff Pullar and all those, and he would bowl at us and when somebody was out, say Simpson was out, we'd put down Pullar and maybe bowl Trueman, and that's how we really started. We played hours on that piece of strip there. It was good practice, but the trouble was we were bowling uphill all the time, and when we maybe got onto flat pitches we tended to overpitch. I mean, we just really put all our effort to throw it up that hill there.

45

I probably played at the Spout when I was about eleven. I wanted to play, you know, I used to come and watch them play against teams and think, well, it could be me up there, and when they asked me to play, I was chuffed about it; but I felt nervous anyway because you think there's a lot of pressure on you, and if a catch comes and you drop it, you think you let the side down. You've just got to do your best, you know, you're nervous anyway until you settle into the side.

Last season we played in the Cup semi-final, and then the captain – I was vice-captain – for two or three seasons – and then the captain couldn't play because he was harvesting, and asked me to take over. We won the Cup, and then at the meeting they voted – the captain didn't come again – and so they just voted me to be captain and I accepted, you know.

John Ainsley: What they're short of at Spout House is practice. We used to get finished milking and our supper's about seven o'clock, straight at Spout House to play cricket, then a gill or two, then back home again. They're mainly farm lads that we've got round here and they just haven't time. You've got to look after your farm, if you're a cricketer.

David Bean: On 26 June the season's play stopped abruptly for Spout House. The hay had to be got in. They finished the season eighth in the eight-strong Faversham League.

* * *

An Outback Cricket Match, Australia
Reginald L. Ottley

Home Service, June 1961
It was close to sundown – you could see the shadows growing long under the coolabahs. As I swung up onto my saddle Bill Giddons rubbed his ear. He was manager of Box Creek station, and I'd been helping him and his off-sider, Dudley, clean out a silted water pump. 'Ya' know, Reg,' he said, 'I forgot to mention it, but we're playing a match the Sunday after next. How about bein' in it?' Plus being a manager, Bill was also captain of the local cricket team, drawn from sheep and cattle stations within a radius of fifty miles.

Not being much of a cricketer I rubbed an ear too; but Bill went on to say that he'd been watching me all day and he 'reckoned I had a pretty good arm, with curve to the shoulder, an' I ought t'be able to belt down a fast one'. I tried to explain that I knew nothing of the niceties, such as 'spinning and breaking', but Bill wouldn't listen. 'Just belt 'er down,' he told me, 'an' let 'em duck. While they got their heads down they ain't scoring.' As an afterthought he added that the match would be played at Ivanhoe, a hundred miles to the westward; he would pick me up in his car at five o'clock on the Sunday morning. 'An' not to worry about tucker. The married men an' their wives'll supply that. An' the grog, too.' When I left him, Bill was sitting on a log, side by side with Dudley, working out the team. I was definitely down as a bowler.

The next day, home on Moon-Bah, I told 'Old Jack', the blacksmith, I was going to play in the coming match at Ivanhoe. He combed a hand through his whiskers before passing comment; the other hand swung on the bellows, showering sparks from his glowing fire. He had a length of rod iron rammed in the blazing middle. 'It's a game', he said, 'I ain't never played. Could never see much to it. She's right for a lad like you. But a grown man ought to have more to 'im.' After he'd said it, he spat in the fire and hammered on the anvil. Sparks sizzled and splattered as I ducked out through the doorway. The art of living with 'Old Jack' was to know when you weren't wanted.

But when I told Ken, the boss, he had a different outlook. 'It'll do ya' good,' he told me. 'Give ya' a chance to meet the neighbours. Howabout whites? Have ya' got any or do ya' need a set? Ya' won't want to be odd man out.' In the Bush great store is placed on doing the right thing at the right time. My nearest approach to the right garb was a pair of weathered grey flannels. When I told Ken this, he kicked a toe in the dust. 'Don't worry,' he said, 'I'm going to Yarrandah in a day or two, I'll see what I can do.' The upshot was, I came home one night, saddle-tired and dusty, to find a brand-new set of flannels, shirt and plimsoles spread on my bunk. When I thanked Ken, he scraped his boot-toe again and told me to 'forget it. I owe ya' more than that.' He was referring back to a month or two before, when I'd killed a snake that was squared up close to his wife. Ken'd been ill at the time.

On the Sunday, Bill and Dudley arrived before dawn had spread its greyness. The time was nearer four than five, but I was already dressed, stiff-legged in my new whites, and drinking tea with Old Jack in the blacksmith's shop. He'd cut a wedge-shaped hunk from the cook's 'brownie' the night before. It went down well with that early morning mug of thick, black, steaming tea. You could see the firelight glitter on Old Jack's spectacles as he told me to 'get it into ya'. It'll stop ya' ribs from sticking.'

The trip to Ivanhoe took two to three hours; Bill spared neither tyre nor piston. He drove his old car with the zest of a man who loves cricket. 'It'll be a great game,' he repeated every few miles to Dudley and me. 'The grog'll be good too, once we've soaked it in a bit of wet.' At a bore on Big Wiloona he eased the old engine to a jumpy, panting halt; you could hear the bonnet rattle as the big ends harshly slapped. 'Another mile,' Bill said, 'an' she'd blow. She's as dry as a duck in sand. Give her a drink while I keep the engine coughing.' As Dudley knocked off the radiator cap, I dipped a billy in the bore-water tank. I turned in time to see him dodge a jet of scalding steam; it arced in a rainbow mist, tinted by the distant sun. When it settled, I dribbled water into the radiator, to avoid cracking the block. Bill gave advice from his seat. Finally he said, 'Cap 'er, an' hop in. She'll be right now. There's only another twenty miles.'

By the time we feathered dust through the one main street of Ivanhoe, the sun was really fiery; sweat plastered our shirts to our backs. On a clay-pan, just past the town, we clambered from the car to join the crowd already gathered. Bill's first job was to hoist a beer crate from his car boot and carry it across to a mound of similar crates. One man with a fire-fighting tank on his trunk squirted water on the mound; two other men lovingly spread wet sacks. They covered each bottle with individual care. Nearby, under a clump of gidgee trees, the ladies fluttered about with picnic baskets; men set up trestle tables for them. A hawk-faced station owner and a fluffy-haired girl sat on the running board of a big, old-fashioned Rolls-Royce. They were there to act as scorers. As Bill said, everything was right down to the last detail. He wasted no time in organising our team.

Another Bill captained the opposing side; he was owner of a property to the south-west of Moon-Bah, and reported to be a good cricketer. Our Bill told me to watch him, and if he looked like getting set to 'belt down a few on his off side. He's got a gammy leg. A horse dragged 'im once an' his foot's never been right since.'

The two captains tossed. Our Bill won. He made a show of glancing at the sun glare in the eyes, but we knew he would do the obvious – bat first, while the men were fresh and the beer untouched. He elected to do this, and we trooped across to the shade, leaving our opponents to take their field positions.

Dudley, partnered by a horse-breaker from Mount Hope, went in to bat first. The horse-breaker stood away from the wicket and slammed at every ball that came within range. Dudley, who came from Sydney, played quite a stylish game. When the horse-breaker mishit and knocked down his own wicket, the score was somewhere around twelve. Bill followed, and almost made a stand with Dudley, but was caught by Phil Harris, the local mail-coach driver. From there on the fall of wickets was fairly rapid. I went in seventh and scored six or seven. Bill was pleased. 'Keep it up,' he chuckled, when I came in from the pitch. 'You were a damned good find. Don't forget that leg ball, when the cow gets batting.' He meant the other Bill, fielding out on the clay-pan. Dudley was our star; he carried his bat right through. Our total score was somewhere in the seventies, and Dudley registered over half of them.

After our innings it was too early for lunch, so it was decided to have a tea break. More beer than tea was drunk, and our side were squint-eyed when we went out to field. By then the clay-pen gleamed redly under the fierce sun. For several overs Bill and another man did the bowling. Dudley played wicket-keeper and I fielded on the boundary, close to a clump of salt-bush – it was one of the boundary markers. When the other Bill rolled, hoppy-legged, out to bat, our Bill tossed me the ball. 'Awlright,' he whispered, when I stood close. 'Now you have a go. How d'ya want me to place 'em?' He meant the fielders. I felt the sweat drip in my hands – I hadn't the faintest idea. But Bill was the sort of man who answers his own questions. 'I'll put 'em deep,' he told me, 'an' a couple close to the off. Then it's up to you.' He walked away, waving his arms at the field.

My first ball puffed up the dust nicely, in front of the other Bill. He bashed it, right into the clump of salt-bush where I'd been outfielding. I wished I was still there. The stance of his bat, when he lined up for my second ball, radiated utter confidence; it wasn't hard to see he had a poor opinion of my bowling. In turn, I felt I couldn't let our Bill down. I rubbed dirt on my hands and took a twenty-yard run. Every stretch of bone and sinew I had went into the ball as it hurled down the pitch. The sound of rattling stumps was drowned by the roar from our team. The other Bill stared at the scattered sticks in a disbelief greater than my own. He was a dejected man as he padded back to the shade and the comments of his team-mates.

My luck stayed with me for the remainder of the innings. I flattened several more wickets. The sun was high in the sky when the last wicket fell to a ball curved by Bill. On the way across to the bustling women under the trees he dropped back to Dudley and me. Sweat glistened over the enthusiasm shining on his face. 'We did all right,' he said, 'for a first innings. An' we've run up a good lead. The thing to do this 'arve is double it.'

But the afternoon blew away his cricketing intentions. While we sprawled under the trees, emptying the crates and lowering the heaps of 'tucker', a dark red wall seethed up from the western skyline. In the hour or so that passed before the ladies began to repack their hampers, the wall grew to a towering cauldron of dust, boiled by the wind that was driving it. It was a 'westerly' howling in from the drought-stricken inland. You could see it eddy and swirl, then boil forward again, covering miles in minutes.

When the full force of the 'westerly' hit us we groped blindly, stowing the crates and hampers in the cars. Men fought to hold car doors for women, some groped for beer and cursed. Dudley pulled one set of stumps, I pulled the other. The wind behind us blew us back to the cars. Raw-eyed, red-faced and red-garbed, along with the rest of the party we crouched until the worst of the storm passed. When it died to a wind of moderate force the air was still choked with dust; if you held out your hand you could barely see it.

The farewells were short – the partings swift. With headlights flaring the cars wheeled in semi-circles, searching for their respective tracks. When they found them, they disappeared. The red murk swallowed them completely and finally. Bill's car was the last to pull away from the trees.

On the journey home Bill had little to say. Neither had Dudley or I; it took the three of us to drive the car. Dudley sat out in front on one wing, I sat on the other; Bill twisted the wheel to whatever direction we called to him. At times the dust was so thick we seemed to burrow a hole in it; at other times you could see for five or six yards. Twice Bill hit a gate before we could stop him. But the worst moments we had were in the dry gullies when the banks were steep. I felt like a fly climbing blindfold.

At the Moon-Bah homestead gate I said, 'So long.' Dudley half raised a hand – he was too choked up even to spit; but I heard Bill chuckle from his seat behind the windshield. 'So long,' he said. 'Ya' played a great game. I c'n still see his face when ya' bowled him.' Maybe he could; then maybe he couldn't. As for myself, I could barely see the gate when I shut it. Yet it's hard to doubt a man when he really loves cricket.

*   *   *

Country House Cricket
John Moore

Woman's Hour, July 1958

There were some tall chestnut trees round our cricket ground, and the doves cooed in them every Saturday – and doubtless on other days when we weren't listening. According to a rather drunken colonel who played for us, these doves used to say 'Take more water with it, Arthur', and sometimes the repetition would make him furious and he'd mutter 'Damn the birds', even if he was batting. He was only one of the oddities who played for our team. We had an old chap who was perfectly sane on the cricket field but at other times believed he was the King. He was perfectly harmless, but at tea he'd generally bring an envelope out of his pocket and pointing at the stamp he'd say rather sadly, 'The head ought to be mine.' We'd say, 'It must be a mistake,' and he'd nod, 'Yes, yes, a mistake – but pardonable.' Then perhaps he'd go out to bat and make fifty with the sanest strokes you've ever seen.

This was in 1939, and I'd come in at the very tail-end of something which even then was dying out: country house cricket. There was a squire who was seen in the game and whose gardeners cosseted the pitch for us. All the prettiest girls in the neighbourhood provided the best teas I've ever eaten – salmon and cucumber sandwiches and home-cured hams and all the appropriate fruits in their seasons, from strawberries to pears. As for the cricket, it was a perfect blend of village and club style. In the holidays there were eager, promising schoolboys, and even some Harlequin caps came down from Oxford. But the village blacksmith played too, standing beneath the spreading chestnut tree with large and sinewy hands, ready to catch us in the deep. And believe it or not the squire's butler played; but he wasn't a Wodehouse butler, he was a very competent wicket-keeper, and if you snicked the ball he accepted the catch with an air at once dignified and apologetic, the same way he took tips from the squire's guests when they left on Monday morning.

Yes and the vicar played, and lots of curates. One might with luck have achieved the triumph which a minor poet, Norman Gale, once boasted of:

> I caused three Protestant 'ducks'
> With three consecutive balls.
> Poets may rave of lily girls
> Dancing in marble halls;
> What do I care for a bevy of yachts
> Or a dozen or so of yawls?
> *I* bowled three curates once
> With three consecutive balls!

One could have done it, because the curates were mostly rabbits. They were the kind Sydney Smith had in mind when he said there is something which excites compassion in the very name of curate. But I never did accomplish that remarkable treble, and now of course I never shall. In the late summer of 1939 we played our last match; William pears for tea squeezing juice all over our faces, the wasps which go with William pears, the Harlequin caps which went with vacations, coo-coo, coo-coo, in the chestnuts – ah yes, but the shadows of the chestnuts were growing long and we had a strong sense of that other shade creeping upon us.

And of course next year in June there were no strawberry teas; and some time that summer a tractor roared into the field and the plough turned over the sweetest bit of turf I've ever played on, burying with it something imponderable, a bit of social history if you like, quaint and endearing, burying it for ever so that the corn could grow there.

*   *   *

Cotswold Cricket
Freddie Grisewood

Home Service, December 1963
We had a wonderful village cricket pitch at Daylesford, on top of a hill, and if you hit the ball to square leg it disappeared down the side of the hill and

relays of men disappeared down the hill and you had to watch the fellow at the top to see whether the ball was coming up. I've known a man to run seven or eight runs while the ball was being thrown up from the bottom of the hill. And we had a wonderful chap, the village blacksmith, who was wicket-keeper, never wore any pads or gloves, and he used to stop the ball with the flat of his hand. Never seemed to hurt him at all. Must have been made of steel, I think . . .

Before I went up to university I was under Canon Horton, a wonderful old man who was Rector of Blockley, just above Moreton Marsh, and we had some wonderful cricket matches there. We were playing against Chipping Camden once and a man had been in and had made quite a lot of runs. And you know, of course, your village umpire is a terribly important chap – he can put a side out quicker than any fast bowler can, which is quite a recognised thing. And the end at which I was bowling was our own umpire and I was getting very worried because there hadn't been an appeal against this man – he'd made about 40, I suppose, which is a lot for a village cricket match.

Finally, I bowled him a ball which swerved a bit and hit him on the leg. It was nowhere near out, but somebody from point or square leg shouted out 'Howzat?', and the old umpire's face just broke into a gleam of pleasure. Held up his finger and said out. So I apologised to the man – he knew what village cricket amounted to. And I turned round to the old umpire and said, 'George, that was a funny decision of yours, wasn't it?' And he said, 'Ah, sir, may be, but it was my first chance at 'im and 'e 'ad to go!'

*　　*　　*

HOBSON'S CHOICE

The distinguished theatre critic Harold Hobson, who is just as much at home with Grace as with Gielgud, came to the studio during World War II to discuss the current state of cricket with Freddie Grisewood. Today Grisewood is mainly remembered as an urbane chairman of 'Any Questions', although among his many accomplishments was a single appearance for Worcestershire in 1908 as a middle-order batsman.

Cricket

The World Goes By, June 1943

Freddie Grisewood: 'You can talk about your Bradmans and your Hobbses and the like and I ain't a'saying as they don't cut a lot o' runs – but that's in this 'ere 'igh-flown sort o' cricket. But when it comes to the real thing, cricket as 'er 'ad ought to be played – on the village green – with the Squire a'standin tea and the village pub nice and 'andy in case any o' the players gets a thirst – then there's only one man as counts at all – and that's the umpire.'

That was my old friend Bill's idea of the real thing, but I mustn't ramble on because Harold Hobson is waiting patiently to talk about wartime cricket. Hobson, I suppose there will be some going on – it takes more than a war to stop our national game.

Harold Hobson: Yes. As a matter of fact, Grisewood, there's going to be quite a lot of cricket this summer.

Grisewood: And a good thing too.

Hobson: The Army, the RAF, the Civil Defence Forces – they're all playing. And the British Empire XI's arranged thirty-six matches.

Grisewood: Where?

Hobson: In London chiefly, and round about. To save travelling. They must have been listening to your Fuel Flashes.

Grisewood: And remembering. That's the important thing. Are people beginning to think about cricket *after* the war, and what it'll be like then?

Hobson: Well, it's hard to make any definite decision, you know, because – well, the war looks like going on for some time yet. But you can't prevent yourself from speculating and wondering. Last summer at Lord's I had several talks with people like Mr Stanley Christopherson, the President of the MCC, and Nigel Haig of Middlesex, and the Yorkshire captain, Brian Sellars. And it's evident that what's going to come after the war is a very important problem as far as cricket's concerned. There are probably six or eight Yorkshire players, for example, who'll not play again in county cricket; they're too old. Obviously Yorkshire can't let peacetime cricket come on them again when they've only half a team, and not think about how they're going to meet the situation. And the other counties have got more or less the same kind of difficulty. And then there's the question of amateurs.

Grisewood: Oh, what's wrong with amateurs?

Hobson: Nothing at all. You were one yourself, weren't you? Amateurs have done a great deal for cricket. They've given some of the finest play. But I've found quite a lot of anxiety in the highest cricketing quarters as to whether amateurs will be able to carry on after the war. Will anyone be rich enough to be able to play cricket except as a professional? The other day a very well-known amateur told me he reckoned he'd lost £4000 in playing cricket – it had cost him £200 a year, and he'd been playing for twenty years. Now, as a professional in that time he'd have made about £8000. You see, that means a difference of £12,000 – it's a lot of money for having your initials printed in front of your name on the score sheet.

Grisewood: The remedy seems simple enough. Can't amateurs become professionals? They're good enough, aren't they?

Hobson: Many of them are. But how are they going to be paid? Yorkshire can afford a practically all-professional team. But Yorkshire has 5000 paying members. What about the poorer counties? How are they going to *afford* a team of professionals? They've a hard enough job making ends meet as it is.

Grisewood: Yes, I see the difficulty. Cricket's like the theatre. There's always something wrong with it; but it always pulls through.

Hobson: As a matter of fact, it's pulling through pretty well in this war. The matches at Lord's and other places raise big sums of money for war charities.

Grisewood: There are big changes, of course, at Lord's, from before the war?

Hobson: Well, you can get anywhere except in the Pavilion for sixpence. And there was a heavy bomb on the top side of the ground. Fortunately it was very muddy, and it buried itself fairly effectively and didn't injure the stand. The Members' luncheon room in the Pavilion is a NAAFI canteen. Nearly the whole place has been requisitioned. The valuable paintings in the Long Room were moved into safer quarters to avoid the blitz. Yes, the war brought quite a lot of changes.

Grisewood: And in the way the game's played, too.

Hobson: You mean one-day matches, and that sort of thing?

Grisewood: Not only that. But hasn't cricket been sharpened up? Last summer several games went on at Lord's when it was actually raining. And players seem to come out much more on time.

Hobson: Yes, the MCC's very keen on time just now.

*   *   *

What about it, batsmen?
Harold Hobson

Forces Programme, October 1944

I'd like to suggest two things. First, that it's a tough world for a bowler. And second, the war gives a magnificent opportunity – one we hope won't occur again – for improving cricket. And I don't mean by altering the rules, either. Oh no, I simply mean by improving play.

Let's look at it this way for a moment. At the back of the house of a friend of mine there is – what perhaps you'd expect there to be – a garden. Not a large garden, you know, but a pleasant lawn – two lawns, in fact, both agreeably cut and rolled, and bounded by a neat hedge. And on the other side of this hedge there's our village cricket ground. Not a very large ground, perhaps, but very pleasant, with its wooden pavilion underneath the elms, and its black scoreboard with white letters, and a few dozen camp chairs for the spectators.

Well, about six weeks ago last Saturday, we – I say we out of local patriotism, you understand, because to represent our village is one of the many honours in life that have escaped me – well, we were playing one of the smaller public schools. Our opponents produced a batsman who was really of the first class – a tall, lithe fellow – I can't imagine how so big a chap came from so small a school. He didn't give us any time to puzzle the question out. He just smashed our bowling all over the place. He drove, he cut, he pulled, he hit very powerfully on the leg side, he even hit one ball right out of the ground, and all through he was a positive model of elegance and grace. In fact, he played one of the finest innings we've ever been up against. When he went in his school needed 135 runs to win, and he hit the 135th run with a boundary that took his own score to 98. You see the significance of that – though he played so fine an innings he missed scoring a century. We sent him down a few extra balls of course, and he'd no difficulty in topping the hundred. But that's not quite the same thing as making a century before the game's over. Tough luck, wasn't it?

55

Now the fellows *I* feel sorry for are the bowlers. Because, by a queer development of cricket, *they* don't get fair play. Just think about that innings. It looked splendid in the sunshine, and it *was* splendid too. But do you realise there wasn't a single thing in it more modern than 1850?

This batsman drove length balls on the half-volley. Well, that's a trick about 130 years old. It was discovered by a man called John Hammond. He was a wicket-keeper. Till Hammond came on the scene Lord Frederick Beauclerk – who organised the first Gentlemen versus Players match in 1806 – sent down slow length balls that looked simple, 'home and easy' stuff, but which batsmen found quite unplayable. But not Hammond. Hammond stepped out of his wicket, turned them into half-volleys, and drove them good and hard. The first ball he treated in this way flew past Lord Frederick's ear at such a speed that he never afterwards recovered his nerve. Every time a batsman today jumps down the pitch to drive he's merely doing something that was done for the first time about the date of the Battle of Trafalgar.

But our schoolboy opponent also cut the ball. He cut very gracefully. This is a beautiful stroke when played as he played it – in fact, for those who rank beauty above strength it's the finest stroke of all. But it, too, is a very old stroke – about as old as Hammond's drive. The first batsman to cut properly was called Beldham, William Beldham. He appeared for the Players in the 1806 Gentlemen v. Players game I've just mentioned. He used to play for the famous Hambledon Cricket Club on Broadhalfpenny Down in Hampshire. For thirteen successive seasons he averaged – on unprepared pitches, mind you – more than forty runs a game. And, as I say, he was the first cricketer to cut a ball.

Well, what about leg-hitting, and pulling, and ease and grace and style? And knocking balls out of the ground? They're all either early Victorian, or earlier still. Parr, in the middle of the nineteenth century, brought leg-hitting pretty near perfection. And the inventor of the pull, the biggest scoring stroke of all, was – not Uncle Tom Cobley, but somebody almost as surprising. It was Julius Caesar. This Julius Caesar was an Englishman, a nervous little fellow. He played for Surrey, and was always frightened that if he failed in a single innings he'd be dropped out of the team. He began playing in 1849.

Big hitting? William Ward, a director of the Bank of England, was the first man to hit a ball out of Lord's. He did it about 1810 with a bat weighing four pounds. Thomas Lord had made a bet for £20 that nobody could lift the ball out of his ground. I'm sorry to say that when Ward did it, he refused to pay up. Perhaps he thought the Bank of England ought to do it!

And as for elegance and grace, they weren't invented by Ranjitsinhji and Woolley – not by a long chalk. This man Beldham I've mentioned – the man who invented the cut about the time of the French Revolution – he knew all about style. He made so perfect a picture at the wicket that someone who often watched him play exclaimed that 'it was a study for Phidias to see

Beldham rise to strike; the grandeur of the attitude, the settled composure of the look, the piercing lightning of the eye, the rapid glance of the bat, were electrical. Men's hearts throbbed within them, their cheeks turned pale and red. Michelangelo should have painted him.' Well, you couldn't say very much about Hobbs himself, could you?

So you see, in this very fine innings there wasn't anything that wasn't really old-fashioned. All the tricks in it were old stuff. They might have been familiar to Charles Dickens or Queen Victoria. They've been polished up, of course, since then, but essentially they remain old.

That might be said of a good deal of the bowling, too. A man called Boxall, a friend of Beldham's, discovered how to make the ball break, and Beauclerk and his colleagues knew all about keeping a good length. But they couldn't bowl a googly, and they weren't very sure about swerve. It was George Hirst of Yorkshire, that indomitable man, who introduced the swerve into cricket. He was practising one day in 1901 when he discovered that he could make the ball swerve. He isn't very illuminating on the matter himself, because when asked how he came to discover swerve, he merely said, 'When Ah got a bit o' sense.' The season of 1901 was very dry, but with this new trick of his Hirst took 183 wickets for 15 runs apiece. I've seen Hirst send down a ball which when it left his hand looked perfectly straight, but when it got to the wicket it was like a good throw-in from cover-point. That was at Sheffield, where the air is heavier than in the south, and there's therefore a great deal of atmospheric resistance to the seam on the ball.

During all that season of 1901, B. J. T. Bosanquet was experimenting in private with the googly. When he was at Oxford he amused himself with an indoor game in which he found that he could put an off-break onto a tennis ball with a leg-break action. Then a little later he introduced his googly with terrific effect, as we all know.

So bowling, you see, has fairly modern ideas in it. At any rate, it *has* some things that the Victorians didn't know about. It's kept pace with the times more than batting has. And yet – and this is progressive – batting averages go on rising and rising. As I said at the beginning, this is a tough world for the bowler. Why, 120 years ago, when Frederick Beauclerk was the finest batsman the world had ever known, his average was only about 27 runs an innings. He played first-class cricket for thirty years, and in all that time he made no more than nine centuries. C. B. Fry scored six centuries in success-ive innings. Beauclerk scored only 8000 runs all told; Fry scored more than 10,000 runs in five years. Gilbert Jessop, against the West Indies, once scored 157 runs between half-past three and half-past four. Altogether Fry made 30,000 runs for an average of 48, and Hobbs's average is about the same.

Well, why is it that bowling, which is the more adventurous and progress-ive side of cricket, gets the thick end of the stick like this? There are lots of reasons. One of them, of course, is the excessive care with which pitches are prepared. Another is the dull, unenterprising use that batsmen make of their pads. And another is the uproar and criticism that bowlers always seem to have to face when they introduce any new ideas. You remember what happened about bodyline? Well, that isn't the only time that bowlers have got rapped over the knuckles for trying new methods of taking wickets.

In 1822 a man called John Willes, of Sutton Valence, was no-balled at Lord's for raising his arm when bowling. He rode out of the ground and never played again. In 1862 Willsher of Kent was no-balled, this time at the Oval, for the same reason. All the Kent men except a couple of amateurs left the ground in protest. It wasn't until this incident that the MCC allowed the rules to be altered on this point.

Of course, you have to remember that in bowling it's enterprise that gets wickets. But in batting it isn't enterprise so much as doggedness that makes for high averages. And the County Championship table puts an obligation on batsmen, especially professional batsmen, to get the biggest scores they can. If they take risks they are likely to lose their place in the team. I remember, some years ago, a match between Yorkshire and Lancashire at Bramall Lane. Lancashire, as I recall, had made 307, and Yorkshire, with nine wickets down, were about 300. Then the last man, Waddington, went in. The score rose to 306. Then Waddington, instead of playing carefully, opened his shoulders, hit out, and missed the ball. The ball, however, didn't miss his stumps, and Yorkshire were behind on the first innings. I'm glad, as a Yorkshireman, to say that Yorkshire won the game next day. But that night in Sheffield Waddington wasn't very popular. In fact, soon after he was dropped from the Yorkshire team. Batsmen, you see, in the ordinary course of things can't afford to take risks. Perhaps that's why batting isn't as inventive as bowling.

But at the moment there isn't any county championship. There aren't any first-class tables of averages. There are no professional penalties for enterprises that don't come off. In fact, this season has been an ideal time for experiment. An ideal time for batsmen to show that they have brains and imagination just as good as bowlers. Well, there'll be another chance next season. So come along, batsmen, show us what you can do.

*   *   *

Lucky Dip
Harold Hobson

Forces Programme, April 1942

Propped up against the foot of the microphone here, there's an oblong piece of paper. It's not very big, it's about the size of a visiting card – no, I think it's a bit bigger – and it's coloured grey. And on the top it says 'Lancashire Cricket Club'. The words are printed in heavy black letters that look very official. And underneath it goes on: 'The Only Rules necessary for Players in the County Eleven are that they shall neither have been born, or reside in Lancashire'.

I think that's odd. And it goes on, even more mysteriously, 'Sutton-in-Ashfield men will have the preference'. Just that. No more. There's no explanation of any sort why men from Sutton-in-Ashfield – which isn't in Lancashire, anyway – should be so popular there. This paper hasn't a date, but it was obviously long before *my* time. I suppose it's some sort of a joke against Lancashire. Still, I wish I knew what it all meant.

I got this paper in the Charing Cross Road last week. I went into a second-hand bookshop to look over the shelves to see if I could find anything interesting about cricket. Well, there were the usual things – Ranjitsinhji's 'Jubilee Book', a life of W. G. Grace, Pycroft's *Oxford Memories*, and so on. Then the bookseller said to me rather unexpectedly, 'I've got something in the back of the shop I think'll interest you.' And he went to fetch it.

He came back with a brown-paper parcel. It looked as though it might be a framed picture, tied up with string. And that's just what it turned out to be – a framed picture of the Australian Cricket XI that came to this island in 1899. It's brown and fading now, but you can still see quite plainly that eight of the eleven players are wearing heavy moustaches. But one young man – young then, forty-three years ago – lying on the ground in front of the others, is clean-shaven. He's signed the picture with his autograph. But though he died in 1915 at the age of thirty-seven, I think some of you will recognise his name. It's Victor Trumper.

That's not the only thing the parcel had about Trumper. But I'll come back to that in a minute. There were lots of postcard photographs of other Australian XIs, right down to those in the thirties. And coloured pictures of English players – Grace, Abel, Arthur Shrewsbury – all belonging to a day long before the first match I ever saw, which was between Yorkshire and Lancashire in Sheffield in 1914. In that game, by the way, one of the opening Lancashire batsmen was called Hornby. He belonged to one of the greatest cricketing families that have ever come out of Lancashire. His father's mentioned in one of these papers. It says he was called 'Little Hornby', and not without reason, either. Because when he played his first game at Lord's he was only four feet seven and a half inches high, and weighed six stone with the bat and the ball thrown in. In Sheffield that day I sat in the stand opposite the Pavilion at Bramall Lane, and looked down into the enclosure at somebody very different from Hornby. This was a huge, red-faced man, weighing twenty stone at least. It was Bill Foulkes. I don't suppose any of you ever saw him play. I never saw him myself. But if you come from Sheffield you may have heard of him. He was the biggest footballer who ever kept goal for Sheffield United, or for any other football team in the land.

But to get back to the parcel. Besides these pictures there were dozens and dozens of loose leaves torn out of all kinds of magazines, like *The Idler* and the *Strand* and the *Sporting Magazine* and *The West End* and *Harper's New Magazine*. All quite unobtainable now, and all of them in some way or other about cricket. A few of these leaves were from papers over a hundred years old, but most of them came from periodicals published in the last years of Queen Victoria or during the reign of Edward VII. Their ragged edges and yellowing paper, smudged here and there with a blot of ink, brought back days we may regret or despise, but can never recall – the days of jingling hansoms and the Jersey Lily, when young men wore a green carnation in their button-holes, and the old Etonians were a match for any professional football XI in the land, and income tax was sixpence in the pound, and horse trams rumbled over cobbled streets. And against this background a hundred cricketers in these pages, bundled together apparently without any plan or system, played out again a score of forgotten games.

Of all these people, the man who is most vividly brought back is Trumper. Because, in addition to his photograph and his signature, there is a letter that he wrote. Not, at first sight, a very important letter. In fact it's merely a note of thanks to some English admirer who's sent him a magazine cutting. It's written on hotel notepaper – the Royal Pier Hotel, Southsea, surmounted by a crown, is embossed heavily in red at the top of the first page. It says:

Dear Sir,
I am very pleased indeed to receive the cutting that you were good enough to send me. An uncle of mine has the Magazine in which the cutting appeared. The gentleman mentioned in it is an ancestor of mine.

There is a photographer in Leicester who has taken a photo of all previous Australian teams and who will also take us, and if you would accept it, I would be very much pleased to send you one of mine.

Again thanking you for the cutting, which I will always keep,
I remain,
Yours truly
V. Trumper

I wonder if he did keep that cutting, or if he was merely being polite? No one will ever know. But anyhow, it shows the extreme courtesy of the man. Trumper was one of the most brilliant batsmen cricket's ever produced.

He'd hit a yorker to the square-leg boundary, apparently without effort. He'd catch a ball off the middle stump for four. In 1902, on his second visit to England, though it was a wet summer, he scored 2570 runs. No wonder Guy Eden said of him:

> Oh, he's just a dandy batsman, he's a rajah, he's a toff,
> Widout any fancy feelin' for the 'on' or for the 'off'.
> He just takes his bat, and tain, wid one apologetic cough,
> Sets to work to play the divil wid the bowlin'.

But you see, Trumper – this great man – this 'rajah', this 'toff' – had leisure enough and modesty enough to thank even people who sent him chance clippings from newspapers. I rather like that.

As I said, all the pieces in this odd collection are about cricket. But the back of some of them are the fag-ends of articles on other subjects. And I found these little bits quite fascinating. One of them, for example, has half a dozen lines on Napoleon. 'His great deed,' it says, 'his great deed was *too* great; he brought a continent to heel, and in the process he taught his bondsmen the secret of success. In the school of continuous defeat they learned at last the art of victory.' Yes, *that's* about Napoleon.

Then the Victorians had their quizzes just as we have. On the back of a picture of the 1893 Australian Test Team, with Blackham as captain, there's a list of questions called Puzzledom. A three-volume novel is offered as prize to anybody who can answer them. Here they are:

What word becomes shorter by adding a syllable?

Short, of course. Short – shorter.

Why is a mirror like a great thinker?

I don't feel at all sure about the answer to that. Why is a mirror like a great thinker? Because it reflects, I think? I suppose not very good.

And finally, why is it absurd to ask a pretty girl to be candid?

I suspect there's a compliment intended there. Why is it absurd to ask a pretty girl to be candid? Well, my guess at the answer is that she's sweet enough already. If that's correct, it's a dreadful pun. But the Victorians liked puns.

Then there's a page from a publication called *The Mask*, dealing with the amateur theatricals, the dances and the sport of the Canterbury Cricket Week of 1868. It says: 'If you want to see pretty faces, you should go to Kent, and if you like dancing, Kent is the place for hops.'

By the way, about that date – 1868 or so – things were done in cricket we should hardly consider in the proper spirit of the game today. There was the Hon. Robert Grimston, for instance, a master at Harrow School. In the annual match with Winchester he stood on the edge of the ground and, in his excitement, whistled and waved his arms about, and the captain of the Harrow team moved his field around according to these peculiar antics. We'd hardly consider that to be cricket today. In fact the Winchester XI didn't then. They complained. They said they were playing eleven

Harrovians in the field and a captain among the spectators. Grimston saw their point all right, and afterwards behaved himself.

In fact, one can see the honest sporting spirit of cricket evolving itself. In such a man, for example, as Caldecourt, the umpire. There's quite a modern ring about *his* idea of the game. 'Is there any reason', a bowler once asked him, 'why I shouldn't bowl in the middle of an over a left-hand ball without giving the batsman a new guard?' 'None at all,' said Caldecourt, 'unless you happen to be a gentleman.'

Those were the days, of course, when the bowler had all the advantage. Grounds were hardly prepared at all, and Lord's especially was in a dreadful condition from the batsman's point of view. According to these papers, this lasted till about 1875, when in that year Royle, of Oxford University, clean bowled Longman of Cambridge with a ball that broke back and shot. This is said to be the last genuine shooter of the true old-fashioned variety ever to have been bowled at Lord's. Bowlers till then – till Grace had begun to knock them all over the field – had had things so much their own way that batsmen had sometimes taken extraordinary steps to deal with them. When Grimston – the Hon. Robert – used to play against Kent with Alfred Mynn in the side, he used to take *two* bats with him to the wicket. One of them, an ordinary bat, for dealing with ordinary bowlers, and the other, a terrific affair, much bigger than the usual kind, for playing Alfred Mynn. Yes, Alfred Mynn, whose name keeps cropping up here and there through all these cuttings in this brown-paper parcel out of the Charing Cross Road, and who had what some people still say is the best of all cricket poems written about him [*by W. J. Prowse*]:

Jackson's pace is fearful; Willsher's hand is very high;
William Caffyn has good judgement, and an admirable eye.
Jemmy Grundy's cool and clever, almost always on the spot;
Tinley's slows are often telling, though they sometimes catch it hot.
But, however good their trundling – pitch, or pace, or break or spin –
Still the monarch of all bowlers, to my mind, was Alfred Mynn.
With his tall and stately presence, with his nobly moulded form,
His broad hand was ever open, his brave heart was ever warm;
All were proud of him, all loved him. As the changing seasons pass,
As our champion lies a-sleeping underneath the Kentish grass,
Proudly, sadly will we name him – to forget him were a sin.
Lightly lie the turf upon thee, kind and manly Alfred Mynn!

*   *   *

KENTISH 'KEEPERS

Nobody has really been able to explain absolutely satisfactorily why it is that Kent has managed to produce a succession of world-class 'keepers. Whatever the reason – and naturally the 'keepers themselves have their theories – there is no doubt that with Ames, the prince of stumpers, the acrobatic Evans, and the health fanatic, jack-in-the-box Knott, the county has been extraordinarily blessed. Between Ames' first appearance for England in the final Test of 1929, against South Africa, and Knott's last appearance, in the final Test of 1981, against Australia, England played 402 Tests, and Ames, Evans or Knott kept wicket in 230 of them. Between them they scored over 9000 Test runs and took 497 catches and 88 stumpings.

Leslie Ames

Radio 3, January 1969

Brian Johnston: Well, Les, as far as cricket's concerned you're really Mr Kent. Were you in fact born in the county?

Leslie Ames: Yes I was, not very far from Kent's headquarters in Canterbury. I was born in a little place called Elham, between Canterbury and Folkestone.

Johnston: Nice cricket ground on the green?

Ames: Yes. Well, not exactly on the green, but they've got their own little cricket ground where I used to play.

Johnston: Did you come from a cricketing family? I mean, was your father a cricketer?

Ames: My father was quite a good village cricketer, I suppose. He was a left-hander, by the way. He both batted and bowled left-handed.

Johnston: How did you become interested in cricket?

Ames: Well, I think mainly through my father. He was terribly interested, and my grandfather used to be the umpire for the village, and there was a saying at one time, when I was about fourteen or fifteen, when I played for the village, my father was bowling and my grandfather was always supposed to hear the snicks when the opposing batsmen were batting, but he never heard the snick if I was batting!

Johnston: I'm sure that's unfair. Were you in fact ever coached?

Ames: No, not really. No, I wasn't in any way at all. I suppose when I first joined the staff I was given a few tips and told not to do this and to do that, but as far as coaching was concerned no, not in any way.

Johnston: How did you pick up your technique? By watching other players?

Ames: Well, I was terribly keen, I always used to go and watch the Kent matches, when Kent played at Canterbury. I always used to go during the school holidays. Canterbury Week was always in the holidays, and those six days I was always at Canterbury. Yes, I suppose so, by watching other people. My favourite cricketer in those days was Wally Hardinge.

Johnston: He was a jolly good one to copy. But does this in fact mean that you aren't in favour of coaching a young boy? What would you recommend?

Ames: I'm not greatly in favour of coaching really. I'd rather put it another way. If I see a promising cricketer, I like to let him go on in his own sweet way. I try and give him a few tips, especially in the art of trying to hit the ball rather than on the defensive side of things. But I don't believe a great deal in actual coaching for the potential first-class cricketer. Don't misunderstand me. I'm not exactly anti-coaching altogether. I think by coaching youngsters you can make very poor cricketers into mediocre cricketers. But once a boy has joined the staff, I don't think any amount of coaching then is going to make him a first-class cricketer.

Johnston: Now, you went to Kent I think as a batsman?

Ames: Yes. I went for a trial, having left school, and I was playing for the village and I got a few runs. I forget how it came about, but anyway I was invited to go for a trial and it was a bad day and we played in an indoor school where the wicket was pretty quick, which suited me. And I thought I had batted just about as well as I possibly could. However, I was turned down and thanked for coming, and that was the end of that. It wasn't until the following year when I played for Ashford as a guest player against the Kent Club and Ground, and I happened to get a few runs, a fellow called Gerry Weigall who was the 'skipper' invited me then to play for the Club and Ground against Hythe. Just before the match started, he asked me whether I did any bowling and I quickly said no. He said, 'Well, unless you're a Jack Hobbs or a Frank Woolley, you know the openings purely as a batsman are rather slim.' So I said, 'Well, I used to keep wicket at school,' and without any further ado he took the wicket-keeping gloves from a fellow called Povey, who was a Second XI wicket-keeper, and said, 'Povey, you're not playing today, Ames is gonna' keep wicket!' And I went out and kept wicket in this particular match. We had two good left-hand bowlers and I managed to stump a couple and catch a couple, and from that day on, I kept wicket.

Top left: The inimitable Percy Fender top-edges over the slips. Deliberately?
Top right: George Gunn adopts a characteristic pose in the nets just after World War I
Bottom: Frank Woolley, nearly 52, demonstrates his peerless powers to Ivan Barrow
(wicket-keeper) and Learie Constantine during the one-day match between Leslie Ames' XI
and the West Indian tourists at Gravesend in May 1939

Right: Harold Larwood (*right*) with his shooting partner Bill Voce looking suitably sedate on board the *Orontes* en route for Australia in September 1932

Below: The picture says it all. Surrounded by an alert legside field, Bill Woodfull takes evasive action to a Larwood special in the 4th Test at Brisbane, 1933. The fielders are (*clockwise from right*) Bob Wyatt, Wally Hammond, Bill Bowes, Herbert Sutcliffe, Douglas Jardine, Gubby Allen and Maurice Leyland. The other batsman is Vic Richardson

Bill Bowes chats to Stuart Surridge, the bat-maker, on his arrival at King's Cross with Hedley Verity on his way to Australia in September 1932

Lancashire's formidable opening pair, Cyril Washbrook and Eddie Paynter, come out to bat against Kent at Canterbury in August 1938

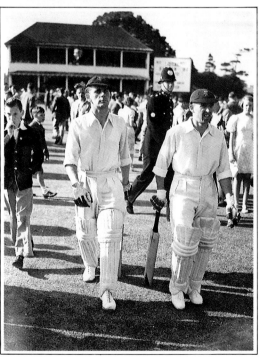

Kentish keepers display their skills
Opposite top: 'I knew you were going to drop it!' Alan Knott lands in front of first slip Bob Wilson in acrobatic fashion to take one of his six catches for Kent against Somerset at Taunton, 1967
Left: Knott practises his knees-bend exercises as a bouncer from Dennis Lillee whistles overhead during the 2nd Test at Lord's in 1972
Opposite below: The agility of Godfrey Evans is to no avail as Ken Archer scrambles home after Neil Harvey called for a quick single in the 2nd Test at Melbourne, 1950. Even Alec Bedser's back conveys his disappointment
Below: A 'bow-legged' Leslie Ames looks disappointed also that Jim Parks has not become yet another stumping victim in Kent's match against Sussex at Maidstone in July 1932. He made 3 stumpings and 1 catch in the 1st innings. Woolley is at slip

Top: A village game on what is claimed to be Kent's oldest green, at Bearsted, in 1952
Bottom: 'Get away with you.' Derek Randall playfully pats an exuberant West Indian
supporter at the one-day international at Lord's in 1979. The West Indies won by 74 runs

Top: A home from home for claustrophobic would-be cricketers in the Australian outback
Bottom: Fred Trueman gets into practice for his desert island in 1964

Denis Compton and Bill Edrich fight their way through the overjoyed crowd in the never-to-be-forgotten final Test at the Oval in 1953 when the Ashes came home after 19 years

Johnston: Do you think wicket-keepers are born, or can you make a wicket-keeper?

Ames: I don't think they're necessarily born. Some have got more aptitude for wicket-keeping, but I think any really good fieldsman could adapt himself to it.

Johnston: You've got a marvellous long line of wicket-keepers, haven't you, in Kent?

Ames: In Kent, yes.

Johnston: Hubble, Ames, Levett, Evans, Knott. Is there a reason for this?

Ames: No, I don't think so really. I think it's just one of these things. We've been fortunate for the last fifty to sixty years in Kent, but I suppose Yorkshire can say the same thing with left-hand bowlers. They have had a wonderful run of left-hand bowlers.

Johnston: There are one or two little knots in the . . .

Ames: Well, the index fingers have got knocked around a little bit, but they didn't trouble me a great deal during the wicket-keeping days.

Johnston: It was not as bad as Struddy's [*Herbert Strudwick*]?

Ames: Oh gosh no, his were terrible, weren't they?

Johnston: All crooked and gnarled. Is it true that in the old days you went on playing with broken fingers?

Ames: Well, you had to really. I mean, you were very loth to drop out, because in those days if you didn't play you didn't get paid. So a wicket-keeper, or anybody else come to that, was rather inclined to keep injuries quiet. Whereas nowadays, if a player gets injured, he very soon lets one know.

Johnston: I think you'll agree there is nothing more agonising than keeping wicket with a very painful finger?

Ames: Well, yes. I kept wicket on occasions when I know I shouldn't have done so, but in my early days we were paid by match money and if you didn't play, as I say, you didn't get paid.

Johnston: Very tough. Looking back now, Les, who was the most difficult bowler you ever had to keep wicket to, the most difficult to take?

Ames: I think all wicket-keepers find the off-spinner is the most difficult one. Perhaps I was fortunate in Kent, that we didn't have an off-spinner. But when I played in representative matches, I always found Tom Goddard pretty difficult to keep wicket to – especially if the ball was turning much.

Johnston: He gave it a bit of tweak, didn't he?

Ames: He gave it an awful tweak, yes.

Johnston: Now what about Freeman – this marvellous partnership? How difficult was it to read his googly?

Ames: Well, to me he was very easy, but I suppose he couldn't have been quite as easy as all that, because he seemed to bamboozle so many batsmen. I suppose it was that I was keeping wicket to him every day of every week for about four months a year and I had no difficulty whatsoever. But I found more difficulty when I was playing in representative cricket with people like Robins and Freddie Brown. Although, in my own mind, I think they did conceal the googly a little bit better than Tich did. Unless it was simply because I had so much more practice with Tich.

Johnston: How much did he actually turn the ball?

Ames: Tich? Very little, really. I think this was the secret of his success. He only turned it two or three inches, whereas some of the other leg-break bowlers, especially Walter Robins and Freddie Brown, spun it more and turned it more, and so did Doug Wright. But then they would so often beat the bat and nothing happened. Whereas Tich, by turning it just a little, used to find the edge of the bat.

Johnston: Now I have asked about the most difficult bowlers at keeping wicket. Who was the best bowler you ever batted against? There must have been several?

Ames: Well, I had what I would call bogey bowlers, but I wouldn't say they were the greatest necessarily. I mean, there was a fellow called Bill Andrews from Somerset who would usually get me out. But I don't think Bill ever played for England. But that hasn't answered your question. I would think generally, on all wickets, Bill O'Reilly. I think he was a magnificent bowler. If he got the slightest bit of help, he was terribly good. He gave you so few bad ones – he was always knocking at the door the whole time and turning it both ways.

Johnston: Nicknamed 'Tiger'. A good nickname, wasn't it?

Ames: Very good.

Johnston: Now what about the speed of Larwood? Can you compare it with any modern bowler now, so that people can get some idea of how fast he was?

Ames: Well, there again, unless one plays against bowlers of the same era, it's very difficult. There's no question in my view that Harold Larwood was the quickest bowler during my playing career. But whether he was quicker than Lindwall's quickest I wouldn't like to say, or even Tyson. I don't think there's anybody playing at the present moment as quick as Harold Larwood was.

Johnston: Was his great thing his accuracy?

Ames: Well, everything really. He was terribly accurate, but he had the ability to make the ball come back every now and again – whether he knew why or not I don't know – but he used to make it come back off the seam occasionally, and of course he could bowl the away swinger. And he was damn quick!

Johnston: The modern generation are a little bit cynical when people go on about the great Frank Woolley. How great do you think he really was?

Ames: Well, I think Frank was one of the greatest cricketers the game has ever seen. I really mean that in every way. Because it's so easily forgotten that quite apart from his great batting Frank took over 2000 wickets in first-class cricket, and nearly all those were taken before 1926 – he took very few after that. But his batting surely must have been one of the greatest attractions the game has ever seen. His technique was different to the modern technique because he was always hitting the ball in the air; when it was pitched up he took a chance and hit it back over the bowler's head. And he would never be pinned down by any bowler. If he was getting pinned down Frank always took a chance; either he hit the bowler off his length or he got out – quite often he got out, of course.

Johnston: What about short of leg stump, which was so difficult to score off? You know, just short of a length?

Ames: Well, I think in modern cricket Frank would find it a little bit more difficult, because in his day very seldom did they have a mid-wicket and Frank used to push the short ones off his body between mid on and square leg – that was one of his favourite shots. That was always open, right up until the outbreak of war, whereas now it's always blocked.

Johnston: In 1950 you were the first-ever professional to be appointed as a regular selector. Did you enjoy doing that, and do you think that our method of selection is the best way of selecting an England side?

Ames: I certainly enjoyed being a selector for the seven, eight or nine years that I did it. It was tremendous fun. Perhaps I was fortunate England had a good side in those days. When things are going well, of course, the players get the credit, quite rightly so. When things are going badly the selectors get the blame. I don't know whether that's quite fair or not but we didn't get a great deal of blame because we had a wonderful run. Yes, I think our method of selection is the right one.

Johnston: I'm slightly in favour of having a sort of Alf Ramsey [*the England football manager*] of cricket.

Ames: Well, they're talking about that these days. I think it's much more difficult in cricket than perhaps it is in football, but whether that will come or not, I'm not sure.

* * *

Godfrey Evans

Round Midnight, June 1984

Brian Matthew had broached the topic of conversation in the middle.

Godfrey Evans: Well, there's a tremendous lot of talk goes on. Naturally the crowd don't hear it. It keeps the interest going throughout a whole and sometimes miserable day. You've been out there and missed a few chances – talking helps cheer you up.

I remember Harold Gimblett was a great chatterbox. He was playing against Doug Wright down at Bath – which is quite a small ground and Harold was known for his hitting. I looked at the wicket and I knew it would turn and, of course, Doug was magnificent on a turning wicket. I said to Harold, 'Look, the ball's going to turn, Harold.' And he said, 'Yes I know, there's only one thing to do and that's get to the pitch of the ball.' Then Doug bowled and the first one went straight out of the ground for six – it was a marvellous shot. I said to Harold, 'Well done, that was great.' Of course, sometimes Harold used to read the googly off Doug, Doug being a leg-spin bowler, and he used to say 'Googly' as the ball was on the way down. Once Doug bowled a leg-spinner and he shouted 'Googly' and played a stroke to the left, and it went the other way. He was livid.

Brian Matthew: One can understand this sort of thing from the social aspect, but what about deliberate gamesmanship involved. Have you ever attempted to talk a batsman out of his sort of stance, as it were?

Evans: Yes, I must say I have. I didn't do very well with Don Bradman – I could never talk him out, he had such concentration. Some batsmen ask you to keep quiet, others are very friendly.

Matthew: Doesn't the umpire ever say 'shut up'?

Evans: Well, it's never that bad. They all enjoy it, really.

Matthew: Let's take a look at the enthusiasm for the bat that seems to be shared by so many top-class wicket-keepers. Why do you suppose that is?

Evans: We have a different view of the ball from behind the stumps – you've got an extra yard which gives you manipulation. When you're batting you haven't got that extra yard, and so the only way I got over this was to try and attack in preference to playing defensively. There are not many absolutely top-class batsmen who are wicket-keepers, they're called run-getters, if you know what I mean. They go for the shots and hope they come off.

Matthew: Sure. We can all remember the times when you've gone in and saved the day with a powerful innings, as indeed has Alan Knott. Both from Kent, of course, and right and proper. That's another strange thing: Kent has produced many England wicket-keepers.

Evans: I think the answer there really is, if you're a wicket-keeper and you've got in your own county the England wicket-keeper, you try and emulate him and have more chance of studying and watching him. So that, later on in life, if you're going to follow him you can see him more often than you could another county 'keeper. I think Yorkshire batsmen – opening batsmen – are similar – you had Herbert Sutcliffe followed by Len Hutton followed by Geoffrey Boycott. It's the same . . .

Matthew: What's the dismissal of your own that you remember with the biggest thrill?

Evans: Well, I think catching Neil Harvey in Australia off the fourth ball of Frank Tyson's first over in the morning when it looked as if Australia could win the match [*3rd Test 1954–5*]. Neil Harvey was not out overnight and he was taking the bowling of Frank in the morning.

I shall never forget. The first ball was a loosener and the second ball he bowled just outside the leg stump. Neil Harvey, being a left-hander, glided it down to fine leg. It went by me fairly wide but it was a foot off the ground. I thought to myself, Gosh, Godfrey, if you'd have been quicker, there was a possible chance there – keep your eyes open, go for it next time there's a chance. Next one was a straight ball, the fourth ball he bowled was exactly the same as the one he played on the leg side. I was over there before he'd got into position to tickle it and I dived full length and just grabbed it off the ground. Because we got Neil Harvey out early, we won the match. I think if we hadn't have done we could have easily lost it . . .

*   *   *

Alan Knott

BBC Sports Magazine, September 1977
Gerald Sinstadt: For more than a decade, Alan Knott has been an automatic choice as England's and Kent's wicket-keeper. His decision to play in the Kerry Packer-promoted matches in Australia seems likely to deprive him now of the chance to break all Test records for a wicket-keeper – most appearances, most catches, most runs. But nothing will impair his status among his fellow-professionals who acknowledge his pre-eminence. Consistency of form has been an important factor in Knott's success and that has been allied to remarkable freedom from injury. Mark Andrews asked Alan Knott how he looks after the essential tools of the wicket-keeper's trade – his hands.

Alan Knott: My wicket-keeping gloves are very, very strong. The backs of my gloves have thick leather – a lot of people like thin leather so the gloves are very supple, but I find by having strong leather there that they give a protection to the hand, they stop the fingers from being forced back, and I like quite a lot of padding in my palms – I use two pairs of inners under the gloves and in between the inners I quite often put plasticine or a little bit of sponge to add more protection.

Mark Andrews: Have you ever used steak? That's one of the old stand-bys, isn't it, for wicket-keepers? Ever put steak in your gloves?

Knott: No. I know Les Ames certainly used it in Australia keeping to Harold Larwood, but it's something that isn't used today. I suppose it's too expensive.

Andrews: What's the most vulnerable part of your hand? Is it the fingers, the palm of the thumb, the back of the hand?

Knott: The most vulnerable really is the base of the little fingers – that's where the ball centres as it's coming into your hands, therefore it's open to bruising. You very rarely get damage there, as far as chips or cracks go. Really it's the end of the fingers. They are the parts that are open to bad injury. The place you get your sort of continual injury is at the base of the little fingers.

Andrews: What about injuries during a game, while you're playing? What kind of injuries have you suffered there?

Knott: You very rarely go through a season without bruising, though you can get away with that basically. It causes a bit of pain, but you can do your job. I've been very lucky in fact, I've only ever had one chipped finger. You've got to find ways that help you to protect that sort of thing. You can tape one finger to another.

With the emphasis more on quick bowlers today there aren't so many 'keepers standing up to the wicket. 'Keepers generally like to stand back to the medium-pacer – take the catch they wouldn't take standing up. There aren't the stumping chances around, so there doesn't seem much point in standing up to medium-pacers because, in a way, you could let your side down if you dropped the thick edge which you would swallow if you stood back. That all adds up to protecting your hands basically, because if you stand up to a medium-pacer, he's got more chance of knocking the end of your finger. But with the standing back, the better gloves, there aren't so many finger injuries around.

*   *   *

DESERT ISLAND CRICKETERS

Whether any cricketer who appears on Desert Island Discs *would choose to take, as his luxury item, a bat, a ball, or a set of stumps is decidedly doubtful. Most probably the tools of the trade have a doorstep reality that immediately dispels the far-flung fantasy of blue lagoon and golden beach. Anyway, shying a coconut at an empty oil drum has a more romantic appeal.*

Two totally dissimilar Test-cricketing castaways settled down at different times, in the prosaic surroundings of Broadcasting House, to disclose their thoughts to the gentle, unassuming Roy Plomley.

Derek Randall

June 1977

Derek Randall: We used to play in the back garden. I'll always remember we used to play morning and afternoon, and mother used to bowl and I could bat. I remember, she bowled a ball at me in the morning and I whacked it straight through a glass-paned window. And during the lunch session, I remember her putting the window in, puttying it round and painting it, doing the lot, and first ball after lunch she came up and bowled the ball straight through the narrow window.

Roy Plomley: She threw it through?

Randall: She certainly did, yes.

Plomley: Was your father a club player, as well as in the back garden?

Randall: He was. He played for the Retford side as well.

Plomley: Now you played at school, of course. Always a batsman, not interested in bowling?

Randall: I could never get the hang of bowling really. I used to practise a lot but I hadn't got the natural ability, if you like.

Plomley: Of course, you went on to play for Retford, you father's club?

Randall: That's right. I played there for five or six years.

Plomley: Any particular Retford innings you remember?

Randall: Well, I remember hitting one bowler four times over the pavilion for six, which was quite a feat for me really.

Plomley: Decent of you really. You could have sent it through the window. Had it ever dawned on you that cricket might one day be your job?

Randall: Well, I suppose I always hoped to be a professional cricketer because I loved playing cricket.

Plomley: What was your job? What did you train to be?

Randall: I was a mechanical draughtsman.

Plomley: Did you enjoy that?

Randall: Well, I enjoyed that as well. I preferred cricket to it, honestly.

Plomley: Something you could always go back to if you wanted to?

Randall: Yeah, I think it's important, that.

Plomley: One day a postcard fluttered through the door, inviting you to take a trial for Nottinghamshire. Was it just like that?

Randall: Well, actually my captain at Retford was also captain of Nottingham Second Team at that time, so he got me a game for the second team and I managed to score a few runs, and they were pleased with my performance so they took me on the ground staff. I did a year playing in the second team and then went on from there into the first team.

Plomley: You had a lot of helpful coaching?

Randall: Well, the senior players in the side helped a lot, and we had a coach at that time, Frank Woodhead, who helped a lot as well.

Plomley: I believe in your first appearance with the first team you went in at no. 8 and you carved up Essex with a very neat 78 that nobody was expecting.

Randall: Yes, I enjoyed that match. I remember hitting Keith Boyce, the Essex fast bowler from the West Indies, four times into the cemetery.

Plomley: And then you became a regular member of the county side. Did this mean giving up your job?

Randall: No, not really. They employed me during the winter. I played cricket during the summer.

Plomley: What sort of sport did you adopt during the winter?

Randall: Football.

Plomley: Football?

Randall: Yeah, I prefer football, yeah.

Plomley: Who do you play for?

Randall: We've got a side together, with Nottingham cricketers, and are playing on Sundays.

Plomley: Now, you are very quick-footed in the field and you've got this reputation for clowning. Are you indeed very relaxed?

Randall: Not really, no. I think I'm quite a nervous person really.

Plomley: So that the clowning is really . . . ?

Randall: It's nerves, I think.

Plomley: There's an instance, I think it was last season, of you catching a sky ball, somebody knocked one up very high, and you took it behind your back just for fun. Now, this was taking a chance. If you had dropped it you would have been in real trouble.

Randall: Yeah, I think the lads think that I have a better chance of catching it behind my back than I have in front, actually! I don't know how right they are.

Plomley: Last season, 1976, was a particularly good one. This really was the year of your emergence, wasn't it? Top of the county batting averages and your first appearance with the English side. Was this also just a postcard through the door?

Randall: Well, I think I had played fairly well throughout the season really, and I got picked for the West Indies/England Prudential [*one-day*] games. I managed to score 18 and 30, and went on to get selected for the India/Ceylon [*Sri Lanka*] and Australia tour.

Plomley: This was what? Four months' trip?

Randall: That's right.

Plomley: There's one story of something which happened to you in Bombay which I think is worth recalling.

Randall: That's right. We arrived in Bombay and I was a little nervous. All the senior players were there and everything, and we arrived at this cocktail party at this big house, worth a million – beautiful place, marble palace. And I remember it led down on to the beach and I sat underneath a palm tree and I got champagne in one hand and strawberry jam on toast in the other hand, and Greggie [*Tony Greig, the captain*] came up to me and he said, 'How are you doing, laddie, are you all right?' I said, 'Yeah, well, the champagne tastes nice, but this strawberry jam tastes a little bit fishy.' He said, 'It probably will do. That's caviar, lad.' So I got off to a bad start really.

Plomley: Well, it sounds as if the conditions weren't too hard.

Randall: Oh, they were really good times. It was quite an experience.

Plomley: And there's a story that the boys nearly got you married . . .

Randall: That's right, yeah. Well, I had a letter from – I haven't told my wife – I had a letter from a young lady and her father. There was a 15,000-rupees dowry involved and she wanted to marry me and the lads arranged a meeting and everything. They wanted the dowry money for the kitty, you know, share out between us.

Plomley: You managed to get out of that particular bit of trouble?

Randall: Oh yes. Nice girl, though.

Plomley: And then you moved on to Australia?

Randall: That's right.

Plomley: The tour in Australia has now passed into cricket history. Now that centenary Test in Melbourne, a great occasion, you had that magnificent innings of 174, your first Test century. And then, once again, some charming clowning on your part, you raised your hat to Lillee's bumpers as they went by.

Randall: Yeah, well, I think I was just glad that he'd missed me, actually.

Plomley: The Queen was there that day?

Randall: That's right, yeah. I remember I got out, and there was a lot of applause and everything, and I was a little bit overcome and I walked up the wrong gangway and there was the Queen at the top. I had to do a quick left detour – embarrassing!

Plomley: Now, you were the man of the match at Melbourne, you got the award and the prize money for that, and you were the man of the year at Retford. You had a civic reception when you got home.

Randall: That's right, yeah. They did me proud, actually. It was a great occasion for myself, and my wife as well – tremendous one.

Plomley: And a special award from the local butcher?

Randall: That's right, pork chops, yeah.

Plomley: How many?

Randall: 174 actually. I'm looking for a few more this . . .

Plomley: One for every run?

Randall: Yeah.

*　　　*　　　*

Fred Trueman

August 1978
Roy Plomley: Fred, whereabouts in Yorkshire do you come from?

Fred Trueman: Well, I was born in a little village called Stainton, near the bottom end of South Yorkshire, just the other side of Maltby towards Bawtry.

Plomley: So you're a country boy?

Trueman: Oh yes, very much so. And of course now I live in the Yorkshire Dales, which is also very country.

Plomley: Your father was a miner, but you don't really come from a mining family, do you?

Trueman: No, my father comes more from a racing background.

Plomley: Horses?

Trueman: The horses, yes. And of course in the late twenties, when things were bad, and especially with the advent of the motor car and horse traffic starting to die away – he was a buyer and seller and things like that – he moved into the Yorkshire coalfields. That's where I was born, in the coalfields.

Plomley: How many were you in the family?

Trueman: Oh, wait a minute, seven or eight of us.

Plomley: So times were a bit tough?

Trueman: Oh yeah, they were tough, but they were happy times.

Plomley: They were?

Trueman: That's the main thing, you know, you always had a good meal and you were always well clothed. Dad was a very conscientious person when it came to the family. They came first, very much so.

Plomley: And you used to help out, by doing odd jobs?

Trueman: Oh yes, I used in the winter to pick the potatoes in the field, and in the summer, well the autumn time, the harvest used to be stacking the old sheaves up when they came out of the van there, you know? Into the old Dutch barns for stacking, and threshing and things like that, even topping and tailing turnips in the winter. And of course seven bob a week was a lot of money.

Plomley: I've been reading your own account of your life story in *Ball of Fire*. You went to church on Sundays three times?

Trueman: Oh, no arguing, yes. The choir in the morning, then of course, when we became confirmed which we had to be and took Holy Communion, Sunday School in the afternoon, then Sunday evening with the choir again. And of course Tuesdays and Thursdays, choir practice.

Plomley: Your father loved cricket?

Trueman: Oh yes, the whole family did. They were brought up on it. I remember hearing my father talking once about my grandfather back in the – possibly the 1880s or something, and he was asked to go to the Yorkshire nets, and when they said what the pay was, as a cricketer, as a fast bowler, he said he couldn't afford to go play cricket, which of course hasn't altered much now, has it?

Plomley: So you're the third generation of fast bowler?

Trueman: No, my father was a slow left-hand spin bowler, left-hand bat. That's probably where I became ambidextrous from.

Plomley: How early did he start you?

Trueman: I can remember playing a sort of cricket on the field when father was playing, possibly at three or four years of age. And by five or six I could bowl at a dustbin lid on two bricks and that's where I learned to bowl.

Plomley: He was captain of the village team?

Trueman: Yes, he was captain of the village team.

Plomley: Now, you played for your school. Your father wanted you to play for Maltby Cricket Club, but they turned you down.

Trueman: Well yes, actually. I went up to the nets with my five bob in my pocket, which was the customary fee to be a member, and bowled a few people out in the nets and was told that there was plenty of my sort up there. So I went and joined a little club called Roach Abbey and went on from there.

Plomley: Now Roach Abbey played Maltby Cricket Club.

Trueman: That's right. That was in the knockout competition. I won savings certificates for fifteen bob for the best bowling performance – I think it was something like 6 for 11 I got or something – I just forget the figures.

Plomley: You just about devastated Maltby Cricket Club.

Trueman: Oh yes. And then they tried to get me to play for Maltby but Dad said he stays where he is; anyway you're too late, he's going to Sheffield United. And that's where I went and joined Sheffield United under the coaching of one of my dearest and greatest friends, who passed on a few years ago, Cyril Turner, the old Yorkshire player.

Plomley: How old were you when the County Club began to take an interest?

Trueman: About sixteen. I was getting a lot of wickets in the Local District and those type of things, like 6 for 1 and 8 for 13, 8 for 7 and 6 for 2.

Plomley: They are rather alarming figures! And then the County Club sent you out on a Colts' tour first?

Trueman: That was the Yorkshire Boys Under-18 team where I toured, and of course that's where I met Brian Close and Ray Illingworth. We were to become closely associated over a great number of years.

Plomley: You had to go to Leeds for coaching, which was quite expensive. Did the club help?

Trueman: Yes, they paid your bus fare, and gave you ten bob. That was in the late forties, and of course what I liked about it – it was always a new ten bob note! That was nice.

Plomley: You were working at the pit by now?

Trueman: No, I wasn't. No, I wasn't working in the pit because my father never wanted me to go down a mine, nor any of his family. But what happened was that Yorkshire County Cricket Club wanted me to play for Yorkshire. By then I had reached the age of eighteen and they wanted me to carry on, wanted me to get a reserved occupation [*to avoid call-uo for National Service*], which I did – which was down the mines. My father fixed the colliery for me, then in 1951 they made a mistake, Yorkshire. On the Monday afternoon, they gave me my Yorkshire county cap – the rule had been passed where you got £5 a week if you were in the forces – so I was capped on the Monday just before tea and I joined the Air Force at 2.30 on the Tuesday and I had finished with the mines for ever. I always reckoned anybody wants a ton of coal, they should go down and get their own!

Plomley: So you won your regular place in the Yorkshire team, and then you went to do your National Service?

Trueman: Yes.

Plomley: But you had a telephone call one day that they'd applied for leave for you to play in your first Test, while you were in uniform?

Trueman: That's right, yes.

Plomley: Where was it?

Trueman: That was at a place called Hemswell in Lincolnshire, where I was stationed. When I look back on my RAF days, you know, they were absolutely fantastic, and I received a phone call from somebody to say congratulations you've been picked to play for England, you see. This was on the Friday before the Lancashire match at Leeds, and so I won't say on the air what I said on the phone to this person who rang up, and I put the phone down –

Plomley: You thought it was a gag?

Trueman: Oh, I thought it was just one big hoax, yes. I mean, I never dreamt of playing for England. And then a bit later on, a great lifelong friend of mine called Bill Bowes, the old Yorkshire and England fast bowler, rang me and told me I'd been chosen to play for England. Of course I knew it was true then.

Plomley: Against whom?

Trueman: That was against India, in 1952.

Plomley: You just about murdered India that summer! [*He took 29 wickets in the four-Test series.*]

Trueman: Oh yeah, I had a great time, yeah. But then I'll never forget that first Test match, because I played in the Yorkshire/Lancashire match on the Saturday, Monday, Tuesday, we had the Wednesday off and I stayed at a hotel in Harrogate, and that's actually where I first really got to know people like Denis Compton and Godfrey Evans, Trevor Bailey and Alec Bedser. They were just great names to me. England lost the toss so we fielded, and the thing that stuck in my mind was would I be nervous, you see? And I was thinking this to myself, as I went down the steps to bowl my first ball for England, and I was absolutely shattered and surprised that the atmosphere of the Test match against India was nothing to what I'd just been through against the old enemy, Lancashire. And I always say now that the atmosphere of a Yorkshire/Lancashire match, especially in those days, about the only thing that would compare with it would be Australia v. England, because the atmosphere in a Yorkshire/Lancashire match was electric. Always had a very, very big crowd. If you weren't in the ground by 11 o'clock you didn't bother to go. And of course there was something like between fifteen and eighteen internationals between the two sides on the field, so you could see the standard of that particular match.

Plomley: And after that First Test, you were still in uniform when you went off to the West Indies for your first Test tour?

Trueman: No, I was demobbed then. I came out of the Air Force in 1953, September, about the 17th, and I went off to the West Indies about December 10th or something, the same year.

Plomley: Now, from what you say Yorkshire wasn't a very happy club in those days. The old sweats didn't really encourage the youngsters, they didn't help very much.

Trueman: Oh, I didn't say they didn't encourage them. They probably didn't help them as much as they should have done. And I thought in the fifties that we had a great side, when you think of people like Hutton and Lowson and Watson and Close, Yardley, Coxon, Appleyard, Wardle and myself. Oh, a great side. And we won nothing. I always thought that we were in two, or possibly three, camps in one team.

Plomley: So, in some ways it wasn't a very happy time for you? Those early days?

Trueman: Oh, it was a bit hard, but when you'd had two years in the Forces you could accept discipline, as long as that discipline was administered correctly.

Plomley: You had a reputation, at that time, for being a little bit of a tearaway.

Trueman: Yeah, I did, but I think that was because I didn't care who people were. I told them what I thought. I just spoke straight because I could never say yes if the answer was no, and I could never say no if the answer was yes. So I probably made things a little bit difficult for myself, but at least I could put my head on the pillow at night, go to sleep with a clear conscience.

Plomley: At one time you were offered terms by Lincoln City as a soccer player. Were you tempted to do the double?

Trueman: Oh yes, very tempted. I would love to have played soccer as well as cricket, but I was asked by certain people in the hierarchy to think of England cricket and my career, so I thought about it very seriously, turned soccer down, and then they went to Australia for the winter and they left me at home without a job. Like a piece of solid furniture.

Plomley: Now a long list of successes can get a bit monotonous so we won't go into all the statistics, but the basic success that you had is that you took over 300 wickets in Test cricket, and that doesn't happen very often.

Trueman: No, there's only two bowlers ever done it, myself and a young man for the West Indies called Lance Gibbs, an off-spin bowler and a very fine bowler, and Lance beat me by two wickets. He played more Test matches than me, of course, which one would expect from a spin bowler, and he took the record, and I think anybody that gets over 300 wickets like Lance did to pass me deserves it. [*Since then their Test wicket haul has been passed by six other bowlers – Botham, Hadlee, Lillee, Willis, Kapil Dev and Imran Khan.*]

Plomley: Three times you took over ten wickets in a Test match. And how many hat tricks in your life?

Trueman: I think I got four for Yorkshire, three against Nottinghamshire, one of my favourite counties, and I got one against the MCC at Lord's, which of course, if you get a hat trick at Lord's, that always gives you great success because Lord's is the home of cricket, the headquarters of world cricket.

Plomley: Great showplace!

Trueman: Oh, I love going to Lord's, I think it's the most beautiful place.

Plomley: Total number of wickets in first-class cricket, 2302. You used to card-index every batsman in your mind; you knew which way he was going to move, didn't you?

Trueman: Yes, I used to have this photographic memory of how to bowl at people, their first movements as a batsman, bowling at them. I used to field at leg slip or short leg, and if Brian Statham was bowling or Frank Tyson or Peter Loader, I used to watch the batsmen, because I was a similar type of bowler. So basically their first movement against me would be as it was against them. And so I had this wonderful memory where I could photograph everything and keep it stocked up there.

Plomley: Looking back, which was the most memorable game of cricket you've ever played?

Trueman: Well, lots of people say to me what was the greatest thrill in your life, and I always have one stock answer, and that is every time I put on a Yorkshire or England sweater. That was a great thrill for me, just playing cricket. I just wish I could turn the clocks back twenty years and play again. Because it's a great and fascinating game. It's a game, you see, that I don't think you can ever learn everything about. One day you've got 6 for 20 against a good side, you think you're bowling against a poor side you'll get a stack of wickets, so today you get 1 for 100, your feet are back on the ground. It's like batting, you've got 150 against a good bowling side, you go against a poor bowling side and think, oh, I should get 100 here, and you get out for 0 or 2 or 3 and you've failed, and your feet are back on the ground again. That's the great thing about cricket, it's a great leveller.

Plomley: Now, in 1968 you retired from first-class cricket. That's when you started to get really busy. You had already been writing for a Sunday paper for some years?

Trueman: Oh yes.

Plomley: And you still do with the same paper?

Trueman: And I love every moment of it.

Plomley: You started by doing a spell as a comedian.

Trueman: Oh yeah, went on the stage a couple of times, told a few stories and had a laugh and all that business, yeah, but that wasn't for me.

Plomley: You still do about one night a week? I mean you are an after-dinner speaker.

Trueman: I speak at a few dinners and lunches and have a lot of fun.

Plomley: And you've written several books.

Trueman: Written a few books, yes.

Plomley: And you've had a television series on BBC, ten weeks' programmes with John Arlott.

Trueman: That's right, it was called *Arlott and Trueman on Cricket*. A history of the game of cricket we did, and we had a lot of fun there. Of course, John Arlott's one of the dearest men I've ever met in my life. I think so much of him and I think he's a wonderful man.

Plomley: And you do some coaching from time to time?

Trueman: Very rarely. Sometimes the lads will say to me, 'Will you watch me, Fred? I don't think I am quite right.' And I say yes. And try to help them as much as possible. That's how it should be, that's what I'm there for.

*   *   *

After Roy Plomley's untimely death, castaways were marooned with Michael Parkinson.

Phil Edmonds

October 1986

Michael Parkinson: You're off on tour of Australia. In fact it's going to last five months. Does music play any part in your plans on a tour like that?

Phil Edmonds: Well, obviously there's a lot of tedium involved in touring. One's in coaches or on airlines. I believe on this particular tour we have forty-two different flights around Australia, much of that obviously cooped up, very cramped, and I think it is quite important to get away from the childish behaviour of some of my colleagues on occasions. So yes, I do tend to spend quite a lot of time listening to the likes of Beethoven, or some of the pop classics of Stevie Wonder or Simon and Garfunkel.

Parkinson: But in the main it's the classics that you take on tour?

Edmonds: Mainly. In fact, during the last tour of India, which was another

4$^{1}/_{2}$-month tour, I took only the nine Beethoven symphonies, so I got to know them pretty well.

Parkinson: Phil, you're christened Philippe Henri. Your mother's a Belgian, your father was English. You were born in Lusaka, which was then Northern Rhodesia. What was it like? What was the environment like?

Edmonds: Well, just to give you a background, my father met my mother when he was teaching history in the University in Brussels. This was just during the war. They then went out in the late forties to South Africa and then eventually up to Zambia. I'm one of five children, three of whom were born out in Zambia. So a very big family, living really in very primitive conditions in the bush in Zambia. Lusaka at that time was very much a one-horse town to say the least. And so we lived out in the sticks and were quite a close family. In addition, my father got heavily involved in black politics. It was a fascinating time, the early fifties right through to 1966 when we left.

Parkinson: Bush country, was it, or what?

Edmonds: Well, it's high savanna land – 4500 feet. Lusaka is not a very big town and therefore one's out into the bush very quickly. We had a house on the edge of town, and then subsequently we had a farm some twenty-five miles out of Lusaka. So yes, we were very much bush people and were very, very close to the Africans, in fact. Our holidays were spent really roaming the bush with our African help, which was very educational in many ways.

Parkinson: What about sport? Were you playing cricket?

Edmonds: Well, bear in mind that the system there is that one goes to school from 7.30 in the morning to one o'clock, and then every afternoon is available for sport. The sun sets reasonably early, but every single afternoon is devoted to sport. And we played sport with all the other youngsters. Cricket, rugby, hockey, whatever. Mainly cricket and rugby. I was at a school called Kabalonga Boys School, which was very Oxbridge oriented. Even up to the early sixties the Oxbridge tradition was really instilled in the locals. The idea of being taught to govern, taught to rule, that was all part of the ethos. And literally every master at one stage was an Oxbridge graduate.

Parkinson: It sounds in many ways an idyllic childhood.

Edmonds: Yes, I wouldn't have had it any other way certainly. And also with my father's involvement in black politics, we had, I think, a tremendous insight into the way a society works and how the establishment works, and we were ostracised from the rest of the white community for a very considerable period. We were deemed to be the Kaffir booties, the black lovers, really because my father was simply expounding good Christian ideals in that perhaps all men should be given equal opportunity.

Parkinson: We're talking about the winds of change time, aren't we? About the time when Kenneth Kaunda was the up-and-coming political leader in the country? Did you know him at all?

Edmonds: Yes, we knew him intimately. My father I think first met him in the very early fifties. For a very long time Kenneth Kaunda, Simon Kapepwe and James Skinner, an Irishman who became Attorney General – I suppose for five years they would have come to our house at least three times a week, basically to learn their politics and the humanities from my father. We saw them literally every week for five years. A very interesting time.

Parkinson: When you mentioned that you were ostracised by the rest of the white settlers, what form did this take?

Edmonds: Well, my father was quite a successful developer, property man, builder, at one stage. He was – I wouldn't say forced out of work, but we found it very difficult to get contracts from the government, for instance. He then set up a soft-drinks company in opposition to the local Coca Cola franchise. That was liquidated basically as a result of government pressure. And really he didn't have a job for a good two years in the very early sixties when the independent movement was reaching its height. We survived on my mother's salary, which was a very meagre one as a teacher.

Parkinson: Was that true of all of your neighbours or were there some who actually took an opposite point of view and supported you?

Edmonds: Well, it was quite interesting in that the violently anti-black Boers, the farmers and so on, were by far the most generous because, I think, they knew what my father was doing. They saw themselves in a different position but they could understand him. They were very generous indeed, and the Greek expatriates, the people who had run the local delicatessens and so on, were always very generous. But the civil servants, basically the British boys, the Treasury boys who came out and made policy, had a lot of influence on the British community there, and we found ourselves ostracised totally. I used to fight at school literally every day for a couple of years, simply because we were the Kaffir booties – get out.

Parkinson: Phil, when you left Africa to come to England, to go to public school here, did you find that an easy transition?

Edmonds: In some ways yes and in some ways no. I found it a bit difficult but, you know public school, obviously you have to work and also there is a lot of sport. So that aspect I found very easy.

Parkinson: I've observed in people from your background that they do have a different attitude towards sport than the native-bred Brits do.

Edmonds: I'm sure that's right. As a young Northern Rhodesian growing up, it was very much part of the school culture and it was deemed that a rounded child was one who was involved in all sorts of things, and not just the academic side. So sport was very important, and in Zambia there is no doubt that the youngsters – and I'm sure that it's the same in Australia – do mature a lot earlier. One has a physical maturity which enables one to go and play with the men. We played very good club cricket against people coming up from South Africa, coming up from Rhodesia, so we were very mature cricketers for 15-, 16-, 17-year-olds. When I came to England I found it very difficult playing school cricket. One would play on a wicket which turned a bit, I would bowl my left-arm spin and the guy at slip found it very difficult to catch it very often. I would get frustrated, and in the end I achieved very little in school cricket – mainly out of frustration, I must say.

Parkinson: I must put to you a quote which I came across of your wife's, who you met at university. She described you there as being an intolerable prat! She said, 'He really was awful.' Would you care to elaborate?

Edmonds: Ah, actually I don't think she's changed her mind for all these years, but having said that, we met in 1972, so we've been together fourteen years, been married for ten. That can't be too bad. I must say, when I met her I thought who is this pretentious young lady, what a pseud. It didn't stop me getting every excuse to go and see her, but I think we've developed a happy relationship. Certainly it's a profitable one too. I mean, Frances now, apart from her work as a translator, has written a book about a tour, the last tour of the West Indies. A very good book actually, a funny book, called *Another Bloody Tour*, which really gives a sort of feminine side or view of these cricket jaunts that you go on around the world. It upset one or two people because of its frankness. I just thought it was very amusing.

Parkinson: You've been a professional cricketer now for what, fourteen years or more? Do you find it fulfilling?

Edmonds: Well, candidly I now play because of the buzz I get playing Test cricket and the frustration of having had a very staccato career, never quite having fulfilled what I regard as my potential, and that frustration really does drive me on. Do I find it fulfilling? Well, obviously it's been a tremendous ambition. However, having achieved that ambition one has to go a little bit further. I think it is now the frustration of not having achieved what I believe to be my potential that keeps me going.

Parkinson: What about being captain of England? A lot of people, including myself, think you would make a remarkably good one. You'd obviously like the job?

Edmonds: Sure I would, but I fear that I fell out with the wrong people, perhaps at an inopportune time. At least it's because of those reasons or that particular reason that I haven't gone further in the responsibility stakes.

Parkinson: As somebody who has toured quite a bit now, have the pressures changed over the years? It seems to me that there's one great difference now and that's the relationship between the press and the players. It's almost press versus players at present, isn't it?

Edmonds: I think that's very true but in many ways I blame the players for that. I've always taken the line that the press are there to promote the game and we've got a duty, really, to develop a relationship with them. So I've been quite close I think to the press most of the time. One has to be pretty hard-nosed about these things. If one performs badly on the field they are perfectly justified in slating one, and one shouldn't take umbrage at that. That's one part of it, but the other part is the introduction of a different kind of reporter. The reporter who goes out not to report on cricket but to report on the so-called scandals involving the touring team. It's a very high-profile game that we play now, there's big money around, and the boys are promoted through the media themselves so they're very high-profile. It's inevitable that any story surrounding the team is going to be big news, particularly in the tabloids. Therefore surely the players should understand their responsibilities to the game, to the people at large, and if they want to go and indulge themselves in their so-called private lives in public, they have got to understand the consequences of that.

Parkinson: One of the things about you of course is, unlike a lot of cricketers, you don't have tunnel vision about the game itself; there is a life outside. You are an entrepreneur business-wise, aren't you?

Edmonds: I must say I do find doing business and participating at a reasonably high level produces the adrenalin in just the same way that P. H. Edmonds bowling to Allan Border produces a buzz. Involvement is everything. One of the reasons that I do become frustrated with cricket is, being a team game, obviously one is watching other people participating for a great period of time. I really now look for the times where I get personally involved, which is one of the reasons, for instance, I like to field very close to the bat. It's only to get something going, to participate all the time. I find that in business.

Parkinson: Finally, Phil, how do you look to the future? Is it to be business when you leave cricket, or do you still see yourself being involved within cricket when you leave the game as a player?

Edmonds: Well, I'd certainly very much like to stay within the game in some capacity. I don't think it will be in full-time administration because I have interests outside the game. But I'd certainly be keen to join the Middlesex committee. Also I'd like to stay in the media; at the moment as a cricketer I'm reasonably high-profile. That gets into the blood somewhat. I think I'd like to maintain that by perhaps doing your job! Not necessarily this one but staying in the media. I'd be keen on that.

*   *   *

SCRAPBOOK MEMORIES

Occasionally in the archives, one finds quite unexpected figures, seemingly remote from the world of cricket, remembering associations with the great players of the past. How intriguing to find that a retired solicitor from Hampstead in his ninetieth year, and a book designer and poet who was once Director-General of the Cement and Concrete Association, had respectively crossed paths with Spofforth and Hirst.

One hastens to add that the third of these dawdles down memory lane obviously falls into an entirely different category. C. B. Fry made a career in doing the unexpected and was hardly remote from anything, let alone cricket.

A Cricket Memory – Spofforth
D'Oyly Munro

Home This Afternoon, June 1966

Spofforth didn't like having catches missed off him. And one match soon after I joined, I was skippering the side and Spofforth was the bowler.

He was rather unfortunate that day because the slips missed one or two catches and he became very despondent. And as we were walking into lunch, I went up to him and said, 'Dear Spoff, I expect in Australia, even your wonderful Australians miss catches off you sometimes.' And he said, 'No, never, I coach them my style.' 'Did you? You tell me. What did you do? I'll buy it.' 'Well,' he said, 'in the part of Australia that I come from we've got hedgerows, and on a Sunday I used to take out a packet of stones in my pocket and I walked on the one side of the hedges and they walked on the other. I threw the stones into the hedges and they caught the sparrows as they came out.'

* * *

I Remember George Hirst
Sir Francis Meynell

Home Service, February 1961

I think the most gentlemanly thing that has ever happened to me in all my life came to me from a professional cricketer – George Hirst, the great George Hirst. He had his benefit when I was at preparatory school and I sent him half-a-crown for his benefit and that was a hell of a lot of money. I also asked him how to make the ball swerve. And he wrote back to me like this:

'Dear sir' – this was in his own handwriting too – 'Dear sir' – and you can imagine that was worth the whole half-a-crown and more to a schoolboy. 'I thank you for the half-a-crown, I cannot tell you how to make the ball swerve, hold the ball at the seam between the first two fingers, Yours sincerely, George Hirst.' And then there was a space of an inch and a half and then he added another George Hirst, that I could use for a swap. Now, wasn't that an act of nobility?

*   *   *

The Greatest Indian Cricketer
C. B. Fry

1946

After a first summer term at Oxford, it happened to me to be staying in the pleasant Minster town of Beverley, East Riding of Yorkshire. And, having made some runs in the Inter-Varsity match, I was found fit for a trial in the Beverley Town XI. The ground, though rather small, is well enough: fine turf surrounded by a low, whitewashed wall, with a railway shunting yard beyond it on the side from the stately Minster church.

The match was against a touring team called Cambridge Cassandra, whose best bowler was a slim, athletic young Indian. He bowled medium-pace right-hand, much above the form of ordinary club class, and he bowled most of us out. He bowled me out for 25 runs, but not before I achieved one surprising sixer. The ball sailed over the wall into the shunting yard. An engine was slowly puffing by, the ball landed plumb on the barrel, cannoned forward to the top of the smoke-funnel, and the engine puffed away with the ball inside.

Surely an omen this and even worth counting as a record, though it is not mentioned in Wisden's Almanack. The bowler was Kumar Shri Ranjitsinhji of Nawanagar with whom afterwards I was to be closely associated for a few years on the cricket field of politics. But I did not then as much as know his name.

The second time we met, he was playing for Cambridge against Oxford at Lord's. He fielded brilliantly at first slip but he made no runs to speak of and he was not much as a bowler. The third time, he was playing for Sussex against Oxford at Brighton and had become famous. And I soon saw why, for, like shelling a pea-pod, he waved the first ball I bowled him to the picket fence of the pavilion. A facile flash. The square-leg umpire had to skip like a rabbit to save his shins. It was, if I may say so, a very fast straight good-length ball on a very fast wicket, and most batsmen would have had to hurry to play it safely with a straight bat.

To me the stroke was a revelation of an entirely new technique only possible to a player with a quickness of eye, a nicety of poise, a surety of foot and a control of hand far superior to the best English practice. It was an instantaneous epitomy of Ranjitsinhji's phenomenal powers. He treated the ball precisely as though it were a slow long hop on a slow wet wicket. No *tour de force* about it. No haste. Just a rapid movement of the right foot outside the line of the ball, into the position of mechanical advantage, body upright but poised into the perfectly controlled stroke.

I saw Ranjitsinhji playing strokes of similar quality all round the wicket for the next ten years. But what struck me was the style of him, the supple gracefulness and pliant ease. No cricketer that I know of ever worked anything like as hard, in order to make himself into what he had it in himself to be. When he was at Cambridge, in his early twenties, he used to begin net practice, two hours morning and two hours afternoon, with a menacing posse of first-rate bowlers like Richardson, Lockwood and Attewell, quite early in March, no matter what the weather. And one year, I know, he began in February. Do you fancy playing Tom Richardson furious with the bone of frost in the turf?

But it was not just practice. It was the kind of practice – a species of alert industrious physical study, guided by a peculiarly acute intelligence. We are talking, let us remember, of one whose almost favourite saying was that nobody is so soon forgotten as a successful cricketer. But nobody who saw him on the field in the days of his prime is at all likely to forget His Highness the late Maharaja Jam Sahib of Nawanagar, throughout the Commonwealth affectionately known as Ranji; and he certainly was regarded as every bit as much of a marvel then as afterwards was Don Bradman.

Now it is quite impossible fairly to set one against other players outside the same period. You cannot fruitfully compare Ranjitsinhji and Bradman any more than you can compare Jack Hobbs and 'Silver Billy', the William Beldham of early days whose doings were certainly very remarkable. The conditions and the standards are different. Both Don Bradman and Ranjitsinhji seemed to me to devastate the bowling in big matches more thoroughly than any other batsmen I ever saw. But as I once wrote, 'Whereas Ranji sliced it to pieces with a Rajput scimitar, Don Bradman whipped it to shreds with a cane.'

Bare statistics do not assist in a fair comparison. On these Bradman appears unapproached. But Ranjitsinhji played under the limitations of three-day cricket, and against bowling which beyond any question was much more difficult to treat with cavalier freedom by way of scoring strokes.

I have seen Don Bradman tear the bowling to pieces in astonishing fashion on good wickets, so as to make one wonder whether W. G. Grace in his heyday could have done more drastic execution. But I never saw Don Bradman make two separate centuries on the same day, one before lunch one after, on a rain-spoiled wicket against Yorkshire with three England bowlers of the Golden Era. I never saw him score 260 not out on a troublesome mud wicket and a slow outfield, when no other batsman on the side that day scored double figures, and that against two bowlers who had played for England and a third who had played for Australia. Ranjitsinhji I saw do both these feats.

Still, I would by no means say that Bradman *could* not have done them, so wonderfully competent was he and unpredictable. One is tempted to sink all comparisons and to characterise Ranjitsinhji individually as a miraculous batsman. But that is an adjective which the philosophers would call 'evocative' – a word which merely excites feeling but really says nothing.

Ranjitsinhji's own key question in appraising the value of a player was: Is he sound? And whatever laudatory epithets you apply to Ranjitsinhji, it remains that the substratum of his play and the explanation of his success was the correctness and soundness of his technique. What, however, gave him his distinctiveness was that his soundness was enhanced, and raised as it were to another plane, by the peculiar quickness combined with the peculiar perfection of poise and with the peculiar suppleness of the athletic Hindu.

In a book of mine called *Life Worth Living* I tried to sum up this greatest of Indian cricketers as follows, and I do not know how to improve on it: 'It is characteristic of all great batsmen that they play their strokes at the last possible instant; but I have never seen a batsman able to reserve his stroke so late as Ranji nor apply his bat to the ball with such electric quickness.'

He scored his runs on dry wickets very fast. I was often in with him when he made 80 runs to my 20. It was impossible to bowl him a good-length ball outside the off-stump which he could not cut, and he could vary the direction of his stroke from square to fine. It was almost impossible for the best of bowlers on a fast pitch to bowl him a ball on the wicket which he could not force for runs somewhere between square and fine leg. These strokes were outside the repertoire of any other batsman I ever saw. It was not only that he made strokes which looked like conjuring tricks; he made them with an appearance of complete facility.

That was not all. He was a beautiful driver on both sides of the wicket in classical style. He could also drive hard and high like a professional killer. India has had, and still has, other great batsmen. I have tried to sketch why to my mind the Jam Sahib was the greatest of them all.

*　　*　　*

FEMININE FORM

Even in these days of so-called enlightenment, the idea of women's cricket being taken seriously by supposedly misogynistic MCC members closeted in the Lord's Long Room is not entirely derided. Ande's cricket essayist who proposed

> *How shall we write of these women, brothers?*
> *Cricketers, just like men, be they;*
> *Shall we not, as we do for others,*
> *Make pure gold of the game they play*

has not had the notion, or indeed motion, accepted sufficiently to the satisfaction of most women cricketers.

There is, however, a perceptible, though slight, change in attitude in some male strongholds, and this random choice of offerings covering fifty years perhaps emphasises a new awareness.

Cricket – Woman's Angle
Harry East

Woman's Hour, September 1958

One winter's evening a famous North of England Test match batsman was sitting cosily in front of the fire in his drawing-room. His wife was busily knitting him a sweater in the MCC colours in readiness for his next overseas tour. Finding himself at a loss for something to do, he fetched his bats from his bag and oiled and scraped them. Perhaps the heat and brightness of the room carried his mind to Sydney and Melbourne, where he had fought many a duel with Grimmett and O'Reilly. He picked up a bat and took middle and leg in front of the display cabinet bristling with England caps, silver-mounted balls and Test match souvenir wickets. With a lazy swing he demonstrated his cover drive and leg glance that had captivated crowds all over the world. His wife glanced up from her knitting, looking perplexedly at him for a moment, and then, as understanding dawned, exclaimed, 'Ee, by gum, does tha' bat left-handed?'

Women, of course, know nothing about cricket. But it is a fact that the solvency and continued existence of most cricket clubs depend mainly on their efforts. Buttering little sandwiches in a tea tent glazed with frosted windows with wire mesh in front; brewing tea over an odoriferous oil stove on a sweltering hot Saturday afternoon; washing up till eight o'clock in a chipped enamelled bowl; emptying the greasy water in the field corner among the docken and nettles and refilling from the boiling set pan; bending and carrying till, as they say, 'mi back's fit to break'; and adding, as they have done every Saturday for the last twenty years, 'they'll hev to find someb'dy else for t'next season. I'm nooan bahn to kill mysen in 'ere another year.'

Their *reward* will come at the annual meeting, when the treasurer announces, 'We're £2 worse off than we were last year. We took £20 in subscriptions and £10 in collections and spent £82 on tackling. T'*women* made a profit of £50 in t'tea tent but they broke *four* cups and *three* saucers and t'plumber hed to come twice to put a wesher on t'set pan tap. I think if *they'd* nobbut been a bit more careful we could hev finished all square.' And who would be expected to notice that there had been no apparent purchase of tea towels, soap flakes or scrubbing brushes since the club was formed?

Women, of course, know nothing about cricket! But all through the winter in every Yorkshire village they are told their duties. 'We're having a dance for t'cricket club, mother. I said you'd help in t'cloak room and lend 'em your card table for t'whist drive.' 'We're having a pie supper for t'cricket club, mother. I said you'd give 'em a pie and help to wash up.' 'We're having a sale of work for t'cricket club. I said you'd embroider a tablecloth and give 'em two or three pounds of your home-made jam.' 'We're having a Sportsmen's Sunday for t'cricket club, mother, and we've getten Len Hutton to come and talk. There'll be a lot of folk want to hear him and t'chapel'll be full so you'll have to miss for once that night. It's very rare you do miss so it'll be nice change for you to stop at home for once.'

But once in a generation their presence will be acknowledged. The cup will have been won. To a mighty celebration feast the president of the club, the chairman of the Rural District council, committee men, councillors, first and second team players and club members will have been invited. As the final arrangements are being made, reluctantly one of the organisers will get to his feet and suggest, 'Wot abaht t'wimmen in t'tea tent? I knaw we can't invite all ten of 'em, but we could 'appen ask four. We can put a little trestle table right at t'back of t'room by t'door. I knaw it'll be a bit draughty right under that window with t'broken catch, and they won't 'ear much there, but, after all, women know nowt abaht cricket, do they?'

*   *   *

A Deckchair on the Cricket Ground
Modwena Sedgwick

Woman's Hour, July 1954

Do you know, my very dear husband always maintains that I have no sense of humour. I wonder. You know, I doubt whether anyone can be the wife of the President of the Cricket Club in a small village without having, anyway, a sly sense of humour. When I first found myself in this alarming position – a wife of the President – I decided to take an interest in cricket. Not like one wife of a visiting team, who spent the whole afternoon behind the pavilion reading *The Well of Loneliness*.

Each year when the cricket season arrives, and I am dreaming hopelessly I know of summer beaches and weekend picnics, my dear husband, the President, is nervously trying on his white trousers before the long mirror, and asking if I could possibly let out any more at the back, as the waist seems a little tight; and if I could possibly drop a hint to our gardener, who is also the captain, that – well – perhaps he could, after all, run the length of the pitch, and – dash it! – older men than he still played, and – well, he did make 12 last year – or was that the year before?

But how pleasant, you must be thinking, to sit away the summer's afternoons in a deckchair and watch the men glory in the field. Well, it doesn't happen quite like that. For one thing, there is the *English Summer*. More often, one is freezing in some other village, far from home, for hours and hours and hours, slumped in the car, peering through the tiny patch made by the windscreen wiper. Then, for another thing, there is *the question* of teas. Each year, at the general meeting, my dear husband, the President, rises and says: ' – and I am sure that the ladies will continue to support us so excellently in the matter of the teas.' Yes, teas. That means baking six dozen cakes nearly every Saturday and Sunday, and cutting mountains of sandwiches.

Mercifully, some of the matches are played in other villages. *We ladies* take it in turn to stand in a steamy kitchen, *surrounded by wasps*, while the rest of the world is relaxing in the fresh air. And, being a small village, our turns come round pretty frequently. As soon as the Fixture Card is printed it is passed round amongst us, to choose our matches. There's a scramble – a very ladylike scramble – about this fixing for matches, of which I confess I take my share. I am faintly annoyed when I find someone has nipped in ahead and bagged the local doctors' match, or the match played each year by a team of Westminster doctors, or the match with the Country Club, or the bitter match against the next village.

When my husband first became President and I had to take an interest in cricket, I did see myself sitting languidly in a deckchair, clapping politely from time to time, with my brood of children draped attractively about me. The first sunny Sunday I took up the deckchair, my sunglasses and the Sunday papers and, ignoring the disapproving stare of certain members of the village team, began to read. But soon a gust of wind blew the papers all over the field, and they were followed by all the dogs of the village. And my children – attractively draped, did I say? – well, they are older now, but I have known times of acute embarrassment. My youngest son had a habit of standing firmly planted in front of the largest picnic basket of a visiting family and, with doleful eyes, watching every mouthful the embarrassed family ate. My stepdaughter had an alarming habit of sitting next to an unsuspecting wife of one of the visiting cricketers and spending the whole afternoon in deep contemplation of her, with intervals of searching remarks on the poor woman's dress, stockings, make-up and hairstyle. And my niece was very prone to standing on her head in front of the pavilion.

Then there's the question of our London friends who come for a peaceful weekend. Poor dears, they get dreadful jolts. The luncheons on Saturday and Sunday are always gobbled. There is a frantic dash to change into whites by the men of my household. And the bewildered visitors are set to whitening the cricket boots that have been forgotten or icing the last batch of cakes. Sometimes they're even sent panting up to find the Captain – 'the second house from the bridge, and ask him whether the pitch is all right to play on' – as the other team has rung up to say it's stopped raining where they are, and is it all right to come?

At last the guests are rushed to some village they never wanted to see, or left to find their way, as best they can, to our own cricket ground. There they sink, exhausted, into deckchairs, either covered up in overcoats and rugs because – yes, the ground is rather exposed – or left to bake in the boiling sun. Of course, if they do drop off into a delightful doze, there is the very danger of a hurtling cricket ball.

I have found, over the years, that our London friends don't come down so often. But you know I don't mind, because I find myself madly arguing the point of Reuben's slip catch, and Keith's wonderful six that won the match. Yes, perhaps my husband is right. I must have lost my sense of humour. You can't be interested in cricket and have a sense of humour – or can you?

*   *   *

An Inspired Birthday Gift
Mrs S. J. Waddoups

Home Service, July 1957

On my mother's fiftieth birthday she was feeling – well – rather redundant. And I expect that many of you listening now recognise that feeling, when after bringing up a family, probably through very difficult times, you now have them married off and in their own homes. For the first time in your life you have spare time. Too busy in the past to make any real friends or have an absorbing hobby, you feel rather lost in the bustling world that doesn't seem to need you any more.

Well, here was my mother feeling just like that as she opened her birthday presents from the family, when she came to a very small envelope. Inside was a season ticket to a County Cricket Club. She was absolutely bewildered! After all, she wasn't the slightest bit interested in cricket: never had been. Anyway, as she said later, 'I shall have to use the thing to avoid giving offence.'

And so it came about one fine day that my mother took herself off to the County ground and showed her ticket at the gate. She found that she had the choice of any of the 25,000 seats, but including hundreds of those good ones that are only 1/6d. to the general public. There were tiered seats on the ground floor or on balconies behind the wickets, sheltered seats under trees facing the middle of the wicket, but my mother finally plumped for the very exclusive balcony for lady members. She settled herself behind a row of women, all about her own age, who appeared to be making a proper day of it. Lunch baskets, sunglasses, binoculars – and, of course, knitting! As you might have guessed they soon roped her into the conversations and arguments that they were good-naturedly having on cricket. She admitted not knowing a thing about the game, and was at once subjected to running commentaries from half a dozen voices, and with the players all looking exactly alike, my mother couldn't imagine how those women knew them apart.

Now, although my mother went many times to the County ground in the following weeks, she was still able to get all her housework done comfortably, as cricket is very convenient, with only occasional matches running the whole week. The weather, of course, often intervened, so that one week there might be three full days' play, the following week perhaps five days, and the week after that only one or two. So that it was easy to fit in the wash day, shopping and all the cleaning. Some days, if she was extra busy, mother wouldn't go until after lunch, and probably leave at the tea interval instead of staying till close of play at 7 pm. You see, once one has the hang of it a cricket match is very easy to pick up at any time during the game, and of course there's usually someone who has been there all day to recount anything one has missed.

However, within a couple of months my mother's whole outlook on life had changed. She had been 'taken right out of herself', away from all her own trials and tribulations, and found that there were more stimulating topics of conversation than family problems, as she sat with her new friends and relaxed in the restful open air. And her friends of the Ladies' Pavilion *were* a mixed lot too. Only one was wealthy enough not to have to work, three were middle-aged housewives like my mother, another worked with the Red Cross. There was a schoolteacher who could only get along after four, and then three or four dear old ladies of eighty-odd, who never missed a single home match! Of course, many women members had full-time jobs and could only come in the afternoon, or during their lunchtime, or just on

Saturdays. But they all said how worthwhile it was, especially as they could pop in at any time to see some excellent cricket.

Anyway, they all tried hard to explain the finer points of the game to my mother, who would constantly confuse her silly mid ons with the long offs and short legs, and couldn't for ages understand the meaning of the white and yellow disc. But she *could* recognise each of the home-side players now, and *could* appreciate a good innings or over when she saw one!

Well, mother's season ticket expired at the end of that summer, and as she went home from the last match she realised with a jolt just how much she would miss the wonderful days she had spent at the cricket ground. As it happened, the givers of the original present were so delighted in the happy change that had come over mother, that they had decided, at the same time, to make her another present of *next* season's ticket too. And so she was able to renew all her cricket acquaintances again the following spring, on the balcony of the Ladies' Pavilion. One or two of them, with my mother, often tried other seats in the ground where they thoroughly enjoyed the matches from different aspects. But they always returned to the Ladies' Pavilion like homing pigeons, where they could spread their belongings out and pop down to the powder room below whenever they liked: 'The great thing is', one lady said, 'that there aren't any *men* to cramp our style!' And indeed that was the rule: no male was allowed to set foot on the steps even *leading* to the Ladies' Pavilion. All the scorecards, ice-creams, and teas and so on, were fetched by the younger women.

There was a privileged set of men, however, who on auspicious occasions were allowed admittance. And they were the players themselves, who went round with collecting boxes during charity and benefit matches. Oh, the heart flutterings that went on then, as the idols of the pitch came upstairs, all in their immaculate whites and blazers, and actually spoke! . . . They must have collected pounds and pounds!

Some Saturdays, when there was no home match, mother with her indispensable packed lunch would go by bus into a neighbouring county and watch another First XI playing (her season ticket allowed her free admittance to any county ground in the country). She would return from these jaunts full of the things she had seen and done and the people she had met. In time she got to know the neighbouring counties very well, as many of them had two or even three county cricket grounds for their First XI. Occasionally mother and her friends, along with many other members, would accompany the home team as supporters when they had an away match. And how the Ladies clapped and cheered their own side on! Well, they had gone to support and support they would, in no uncertain manner!

Towards the end of mother's second season she had made firm friends with quite a number of the women, and once or twice, for a change from bringing their packed lunches, they would all troop out of the ground to an inexpensive little restaurant they had discovered and have a proper meal.

And if one of the 'regulars' had a birthday, or had been celebrating a family wedding, well then there would be tea and cakes or lemonade all round. This delightful group also began to meet regularly throughout the winter months, and visited one another's homes. They began taking active interest in the Cricket Club, and in the following years they even stood up and asked questions and put forward very sound suggestions at the Annual General Meetings.

You may be wondering how the husbands fared all this time. Well, you know, provided their usual routine isn't disturbed, the majority of husbands don't mind a bit. In most cases, where the man is out all day, it only means him finding his evening meal warm in the oven, or something cold all ready prepared in the larder. His wife will be home anyway about 7, so he isn't alone for long. And those wives with cricket-loving husbands have little to worry about.

Well, my mother has been a member for nine years now, and no one will believe her age, as she really does look younger at present than she did ten years ago! She has emerged into a fresh personality, with wide interests, can laugh easily, and is in excellent health from the open-air life she leads at the cricket ground. All in all, a delight to father as well as the rest of her family and friends, and it all comes from what must have been an inspired birthday gift.

*   *   *

Rachael Heyhoe Flint

Profile, October 1973
Rachael Heyhoe Flint: It started at a very early age. I always say I used to play cricket with my brother and his friends in the garden. I was used to preserve the flower-bed and to run next door to the neighbours to chat them up and ask them for the ball back, so the boys discovered that I was pretty useful. I wasn't allowed to bat or bowl to begin with, but then my father used to play a lot of cricket and I used to go along and watch him play, and every weekend was cricket to me in the summer and it was rumoured that I could score at cricket before I could even write a sentence.

Alastair Lack: Was that true?

Heyhoe Flint: Well, I deny it now, but I wasn't quite sure at the time actually. I felt that my education was quite complete and that, as I could score at cricket, nothing else really mattered. People assume that because I play cricket I enjoyed masculine pursuits but really I always argue that cricket is a very graceful game and there's no physical contact involved, and you know, if you think of somebody like Tom Graveney batting, or Colin Cowdrey, there's nothing brutal about that.

Lack: It's all timing.

Heyhoe Flint: Sheer timing, and it looks wonderful.

Lack: Do you think there is anything that women can do better than men in cricket, or women potentially could do better?

Heyhoe Flint: The one thing that people most comment upon is the fact that we field extremely well. It's all in relation to the speed at which the ball is hit and this sort of thing, but we played Old England men the other week at the Oval cricket ground in London, and the crowd were in absolute raptures at our fielding – they just couldn't get over the fact that we were capable of throwing 65, 70 yards, right into the wicket-keeper's gloves. And I always say that possibly we are good at fielding because our centre of gravity's a bit lower, we can bend down more easily than men!

Lack: What about close-fielding reactions? Are they as fast as men?

Heyhoe Flint: Probably one of our weaknesses is slip-fielding. We have one girl who has tremendously quick reactions, but I think she is unique in that she can react so quickly in the slips. It might be the fact that she also does judo and she's a black belt to boot! This is why she moves so quickly.

Lack: You are a bats . . . woman I suppose I had better say, rather than batsman?

Heyhoe Flint: Well, I wouldn't say batsman. I think I could pass all the necessary tests – I hope, she cried. I think we are referred to as bats, you know, just in case people aren't quite sure what species we are.

Lack: Yes, the vocabulary gets rather complicated.

Heyhoe Flint: You could talk about fieldswomen and fielders as we call it, so it does get rather garbled, but no, I mainly bat No. 3.

Lack: And several Test centuries to your credit?

Heyhoe Flint: Yes, I have got a few. We are, unlike most women who are concerned with vital statistics, not very concerned with cricket statistics. I apparently have scored nineteen centuries in all grades of cricket, which is from school to club to regional to national cricket.

Lack: Of course, as I understand it it's fairly rare for women to score centuries. Much more rare than for men to score them?

Heyhoe Flint: Well, it would be because we obviously don't play quite so much. We are amateurs, we don't play seven days a week as the poor men of

England seem to do at the moment. We probably play two or three times a week, evening matches midweek, a day game on Saturday, and perhaps an afternoon game on Sunday, so it probably is a little more difficult to score centuries, but I always have been very greedy.

Lack: And of course you have been captain of the England team for seven years, and in that time you have travelled a lot, haven't you? Now what's the team like when it's travelling? Is it really like men's cricket, are you as serious as they are? Or do you take more time off for shopping?

Heyhoe Flint: We always have a good rota going. When we have a party of about fifteen or sixteen, eleven are playing, one is at twelfth, and one is scoring usually. So 14, 15 and 16 go off on the shopping patrol in the morning, but they are always back for lunch at the ground. But we do take it seriously. I think we like people to enjoy watching us play because we are trying to encourage people that women's cricket is an attractive game, and it's no use boring their pants off.

Lack: Are there any particular innings or games you remember on tours with England?

Heyhoe Flint: I can remember a lot, but I think the one or two that I remember more than any were when we were in New Zealand. We had drawn three matches in 1966 in this country against New Zealand. We played the first three in Australia, this was in 1968, drew those three, and then went on to New Zealand and drew the first one, and I thought, Oh God, are we going to have three more drawn matches, what a bore! And we are playing them at Christchurch, and we eventually got them all out and we needed to score, I think it was something like 176 in 121 minutes to win, which is, you know, a pretty good rate of scoring in any standard of cricket, and we eventually got these with about three minutes to spare and it was the most incredible excitement. I couldn't watch in the end, I had gone in and got a few quickly and I had come out, and I apparently was in the corner of the dressing-room cutting my toenails when the winning hit was made.

Lack: Talking about tension, it's probably unfair of me to say this but I think we often feel women are more emotional than men about these things. Do you find that the England team gets very emotional, or . . . ?

Heyhoe Flint: We don't run up and kiss one another, like the footballers do when they get a goal, when we get a wicket or anything like that. I don't know why. We all seem to have a good sense of humour.

Lack: Probably need one if you are going to be a woman cricketer.

Heyhoe Flint: You might do, yes, with all the slings and arrows that come at you for the fact that you are playing cricket. I think you get used to a few comments, particularly from the cynical males.

Lack: What sort of comments?

Heyhoe Flint: Well, you know, do you bowl underarm, do you use a tennis ball? In fact, women invented overarm bowling in 1805, because of the wide crinoline skirts. This girl called Christina Willes couldn't bowl underarm so she invented overarm bowling. Her brother saw it, thought it was pretty good, was no-balled out of the game, and no less than sixty years later the men adopted it as the official technique, by which time, I hasten to add, everybody had forgotten that it was in fact a woman who had invented the idea.

Lack: So women were playing as long ago as in the nineteenth century?

Heyhoe Flint: Apparently the earliest record of a women's cricket game is something like 1745. You know, a lot of people think we came down in the last shower of rain, but we have had an association in this country since 1926, and we've been having regular tours since 1934, but still people refuse to take us seriously.

Lack: You obviously can make jokes and I should think you are not, by now, over-sensitive about it, but why have you persevered so much in cricket? Because I think you do, if you are a woman, have to persevere.

Heyhoe Flint: I think really it was a mistake. When I first played at school, for example, I never even knew there was an England team, and then when I eventually got into the England team, having discovered that there was club cricket and this sort of thing, I enjoyed it very much. I think the turning point came when I left teaching and became a journalist. And suddenly I thought, we're playing pretty reasonable cricket, we are getting very good results, the England team haven't lost a Test match since 1951, and why shouldn't people know about us? Working in a newspaper office I had learned about handouts and press conferences and all the sort of things that encourage the press to take interest, and I suddenly thought, why shouldn't I try and relate this to women's cricket and see if people would take an interest in us, and it's amazing how it's caught on.

*　　　*　　　*

Marjorie Pollard, hockey international, brave batswoman, and enthusiastic editor of the journal Women's Cricket, *was an obvious choice to commentate on the first Women's Test match in England, against Australia at Northampton. Alluding to the players formally highlights the conventional, somewhat prissy style of the day.*

First Home Test
Marjorie Pollard

June 1937

The score is now 220 and Miss Smith's score 49. Now then, will she get that 50? Miss Child has fielded the ball, just running back into position. Miss Belton licking her fingers, taking up her stand. Off she goes. Full pitch and Miss Smith pulled it round. And it's going away on the leg side. They're running two. No it's not going. They're running three. No, no, they didn't get the third run. And Miss Smith has now made 51. And no doubt you'll hear the applause.

Miss Smith comes from Brisbane and is actually a fast as well as a very strong determined batsman. Miss Belton going up once more. Here she goes, over, also well pitched up and Miss Smith straight drove that past where mid on should have been and it's come for four. Another four. They'll have to have a long on out here yet, I think. Back it goes to Miss Belton. Now she's considering the matter rather. Miss Smith's walking back to her position. A solid player this Miss Smith, she's crouching down. Here comes Miss Belton. Over she goes. Oh, and Miss Smith took a terrific wahoo at that. It pitched outside the off stump and Miss Smith missed it altogether and Miss Snowball took it quite calmly, the wicket-keeper took it quite calmly, and back it comes to Miss Belton. She's turning round. Off she goes, swinging her arms and over she goes. Well pitched up again and oh, Smithy, a beautiful shot past point. Three fieldsmen running for it. However, third man picked it up and, yes, they've run three runs.

Miss Smith's score is now 58 and Australia 229. It looks as though they're going to get that 300 that Mrs Peden, the Australian captain, was after.

Australia did and Miss Smith, Kath to her friends, made 88. Ultimately the ladies from Down Under won an exciting match by 31 runs.

*   *   *

The job of the commentator in the noisy sub-continent of India, with possibly as many as 50,000 excitable spectators accompanied by fire-crackers at the Test grounds, calls for considerable concentration and also a voice that can be heard distinctly above the hubbub. Shandra Nayudu, daughter of C. K. Nayudu, a former captain of India, who once hit eleven sixes in an innings against MCC, talks about giving ball-by-ball commentary for All-India Radio.

Shandra Nayudu, Speakerene

BBC Sports Magazine, December 1981

Shandra Nayudu: My father was the first cricketer to captain the Indian Test side and I just wanted to be the first in something connected with cricket. As far as playing cricket was concerned it came on my scene much too late and this was the only field open to me. At least in India, I think I am the first woman cricket commentator.

Peter Baxter: Do you find it a very daunting business, cricket commentary in India? I've seen everyone listening on the street corners with their transistors, and all round the ground you can hear your voice coming back to you. Is that very nerve-wracking?

Nayudu: It is, Peter. It is really nerve-wracking. You are conscious all the time that so many thousands are listening to you. What I feel is, they are finding it rather strange to have a female voice talking to them and the moment I come on they raise the volume.

The very first commentary that I did was in 1977, and I must say that the reaction to my first commentary was rather explosive. It was explosive in the sense that men just could not take this idea of a woman coming into the field. I got both brickbats and bouquets.

*   *   *

In the last few years, and having opened both the batting and bowling for the England Test side, Sarah Potter has attracted more column inches than any other woman cricketer in the country. As a prelude to a featurette in 1982, Marshall Lee went into the nets to face a few probing deliveries from the sinister-handed Sarah. Then it was his turn to set things in motion.

Sarah Potter

Newsnight, BBC2, February 1982

Marshall Lee: In Hereford, where hurricanes hardly ever happen, there's a breeze of change. The city cricket club has signed a local player destined to play for England and bound to cause a flutter on the cricket score. I went along to see why.

Eight o'clock on a winter Wednesday evening in Hereford, and Sarah Potter is the last man in the nets.

Sarah Potter: It's such an exhilarating game, not just physically but also mentally. I always think of it as a sort of chess blown up, and once you start playing it's very much like a drug, you just can't help it, you know, you just carry on.

Lee: Hooked on cricket, Sarah's also into a bit of black magic. At the age of twenty she's writing her first novel, or at least the prose version of the film *Brimstone and Treacle*. For this job she's got Dad to thank because he's Dennis Potter, the *Pennies from Heaven* man, and *Brimstone* is actually his play. What's more, working for her father means she can find time to play the cricket she's crazy about. Signed up by Hereford, she's the first woman ever to join a strong men's city league side.

Potter: I'm going to be slower in a man's game. For instance, in a women's cricket game I'm classified as fast. In men's cricket I'd be medium-pace, and their bowlers are obviously going to be a lot quicker than I've ever faced before, but that doesn't really worry me. I see it more as a challenge, and something that will quicken me up and make me sharper, and when I come to play women's cricket, I'll be that much more prepared.

Lee: Sarah, there's another fear. That you, a slip of a thing, will get hurt.

Potter: It's a fear in any sport – that somebody's going to get hurt. It can be in cricket, it can happen to a man as much as a woman, but what I would say is that obviously, if I was playing for Hereford, then I would be perhaps ten or eleven batsperson, and that the gentlemen's agreement of an unorganised batsman coming to the crease would mean that the bowler wouldn't short-pitch them, so that agreement, as it were, would hold true for me.

Lee: What if they're going for points, and the points are all important?

Potter: Yes, but you see you only kind of attack a batsman if you think that he or she is capable of playing the ball. [*Really!*] Obviously you don't put on a pair of cricket whites to go out and kill somebody. That's not the idea of the game, you know. It's not a blood sport.

Lee: Women's cricket has always been regarded by men as something of a joke, something to titter over. So I asked Tracey Goodwin, captain of Hereford, how good Sarah is.

Tracey Goodwin: Sarah is an excellent cricketer. A lot of potential. You've seen her batting tonight. To be fair to her, she showed up much better batting, she did herself justice there, but she hasn't done herself justice bowling this evening, but potentially she's a very good cricketer.

Lee: What team will she play for?

Goodwin: It's difficult to say at this stage. At her present stage she is likely to get into our second team. The policy through the club is that we have a selection committee and people are chosen on merit, so Sarah will be chosen on merit whatever side she plays in.

Lee: Hereford are actually a strong club, the strongest in their Three Counties League, and they have a long history behind them. Their break with tradition has raised eyebrows round the county, but the hierarchy tolerate their move only because they feel a few Sarah Potters will hardly make an impact on the game. But is it, perhaps, one positive step towards desegregated cricket? I asked Brian Aspital, the secretary of the National Cricket Association.

Brian Aspital: No, I don't think so. I think cricket will continue at club level in its own way, as it's done over many years, and we may have some women involved at local level now and again, but I can't see club cricket changing its trends very much. But let's be fair, women do at this moment play a considerable part in club cricket. Most clubs rely to a great extent on their lady members, particularly as they do the tea week in and week out and help with the social events. Oh, they're a very important part of club cricket, very important part.

Lee: So, in the clubhouse, as elsewhere, men expect to find their women in the kitchen, but Sarah is absolutely determined she's going to be out there bowling . . .

*   *   *

Whilst on duty at the Lord's Test in 1983, Tony Lewis was watching Fatima Whitbread on his television monitor so nearly getting a javelin gold medal in Helsinki. Eventually he had the chance to meet up with Fatima and her mother Margaret, and perhaps surprisingly they started to talk about cricket.

Fatima and the Folly of the Fast Bowlers

Sport on Four, August 1983
Margaret Whitbread: On the way home from Helsinki we quickly looked up in the newspaper the result of the Test match between England and New Zealand, but I would like to say that I feel Fatima or myself could help some of the England fast bowlers improve their speed of delivery. Because their technique isn't quite right, and I hope they don't think we're being rude but it's so similar to the javelin throw –

Tony Lewis: What do they do wrong?

Margaret Whitbread: Their last two strides are wrong – mainly their last stride which is far too long – and they're overstretching which is causing them to fall away to the left-hand side and also putting tremendous stress on the lower-back area.

Lewis: There is a lot of similarity obviously. The sort of bowler I'm thinking of now is Graham Dilley. Have you seen him bowl?

Margaret Whitbread: Yes. I watched him bowl very recently when Kent were playing in the Nat. West, and I felt that day again after watching him previously in the Test matches that he's definitely far too long in the last stride and his speed of delivery could be improved enormously. I'd love to coach him for a few days.

Lewis: Well, I hope he's listening. Fatima, have you noticed this about cricketers too?

Fatima Whitbread: Yes, I have obviously. It's very similar to the javelin throw, and I like to watch cricket anyway, but we take a special interest in watching their technique. I think they could all do with a bit of coaching.

Lewis: A shortening of the last stride?

Fatima Whitbread: Of the last stride, yes. Because it would put an awful lot of speed in the release of the ball from the arm, which would give a tremendous help.

Lewis: The difficulty is that they can't throw the ball, of course. They have to bowl it with a straight arm.

Fatima Whitbread: Oh, that's all right. I understand the difference between throwing and bowling because a lot of novice javelin throwers try to bowl, and I say to them, just try to imagine throwing a cricket or rounders ball, if I have a particular problem in school or if I'm doing a coaching session. Don't worry, I wouldn't encourage them to throw the ball!

Lewis: You've got me worried, you two. You know more about cricket than I do.

* * *

PERSONALITY PROFILE

Superlatives abound. Two post-war England captains, one who 'skip-pered' the side more times than anybody else, the other who has played in more Tests than any other Englishman; one of the most adroit players to lead Australia; two of the world's greatest all-rounders; three of the world's greatest batsman; and one of the greatest fast bowlers.

Peter May

Cricket – A Way of Life, February 1976
Christopher Martin-Jenkins: Who was the most accomplished English post-war batsman? There are plenty of claimants, but a good many of the best judges would put P.B.H. May at the top of the list. What a pity, someone said to me recently, a non-cricketer I should add though a keen sportsman, that Peter May is such an anonymous figure these days. See him walk down a street in London in a city suit and no one would recognise him. Well, that may just possibly be true, but in any case my acquaintance's observation missed the point altogether. Peter May never sought the lime-light, indeed he shied away from it whenever he could, and it was the wish to become an ordinary family man again which had a lot to do with his retirement after 1962. By that time he'd scored 85 hundreds, captained England during a very successful run marred only by the heavy reverse in Australia in 1958/59, and of course captained the great Surrey side of the 1950s. Those who thought of him as a quiet undemonstrative character were right. Those who thought this also meant he was weak were very wrong. Peter May was tough mentally and physically, and the bigger the occasion the better he used to bat. Equally, just because he's faded from the public eye certainly doesn't mean that he's either lost interest in the game or that he doesn't have some strong views about how it should develop. Nor indeed that he doesn't play an active part in administration. You still do, of course, don't you?

Peter May: Yes, though it's fourteen years since I played, I get very in-volved at the Oval. I am Chairman of the Surrey Cricket Committee which I enjoy doing, it keeps one involved and one gets involved in various sub-committees. I am on committees at Lord's, the TCCB Cricket Committee, and I feel it's nice to get involved. One makes mistakes but one wants to get involved in administration and help the thing along and I think we've got some very encouraging cricketers today. I try not to be one of those people who says, 'In my day everything was marvellous and today it's dreadful,'

114

because I don't believe it. I think we've got some very fine cricketers. I just wonder whether perhaps some of them enjoy it as much as I did when I was playing. I used to wake up in the morning and think, gosh, how marvellous to play cricket all day. And this was the way we played it, we had this marvellous Surrey side where we won the championship for seven years as you remember, in the fifties, and of course we had a marvellous run with the England side, which I was fortunate enough to captain for quite a number of times, and I think if you look at the history from 1951 until 1959, we won or drew every Test series.

Martin-Jenkins: Why was that such a golden age, do you think?

May: Well, we had marvellous bowlers, and I think your bowlers win the matches. We had four wonderful Surrey bowlers, didn't we? Bedser, Loader, Laker and Lock, who of course played for England. I mean, we sometimes had four and five Surrey players. And if you've got the bowlers on wickets where you get a little bit of help, you can control the game. We always seemed to get enough runs, just enough.

Martin-Jenkins: You are convinced then, as a great batsman, that it is the bowlers who win matches?

May: I think bowlers win matches, I think that's right. Alec Bedser always reminded me of this fact, and I think as one of the greatest bowlers I ever saw on all wickets, I think this was right. When it does find you out, of course, is when you're playing on a beautiful wicket, when 300 is par for the course and you can't get 300. And we found this when we lost in Australia in 1958–9. Do you remember we couldn't get enough runs?

Martin-Jenkins: I wanted to ask you about that, which is really one of the unsuccessful times that you had as captain. Was it severe batting failure?

May: Well, we didn't get enough runs, for various reasons. I think this is the charm of cricket. You've got to lose sometimes. And we had this marvellous run for seven or eight years, against all countries, and you are going to lose one day. I don't think it's a tragedy to lose. We got a good hiding. They had one or two bowlers with some unusual actions, which I don't want to digress into, that's history. But I think it's a pity to be frightened of losing. That's all part of it. You win some, you lose some.

Martin-Jenkins: Are we setting too much store by winning and losing, and are we therefore too hard on captains who do lose?

May: Well, there is a tremendous amount of focus today, even more than when I was playing – the games are dissected and played back in slow motion. I would like to think that, provided one feels one's got the right side, one's picked the right side, one should support the players. I tend to think that we are perhaps not quite so loyal to our players as perhaps the

Australians are, who when they pick somebody tend to give them a longer run. And I think you've got a tremendous number of England captains, when you look at the number of Australian captains there have been [*at that time 58 to 35*]. And perhaps with the focus on it and the pressure, it necessitates the changes more, over here.

Martin-Jenkins: Isn't this partly though, Peter, because we play more cricket and we have more cricketers and there seems to be a general standard at the top. You could almost pick two or three equal England sides at the present time, whereas in Australia they tend to stand out and pick themselves almost?

May: Yes, I think there's certainly less cricketers to pick from out there. I was a selector for a few years, and believe me, it's a very difficult job. You never go to the right ground and see the right player do the right thing. You may go and see a batsman – he may take a first ball, or it may rain. I went all the way down to Swansea to watch a Glamorgan fast bowler some years ago because we were quite keen that he might go to Australia, and they left him out of the side, the wicket didn't suit him. So I didn't learn much about Jeff Jones on that day, and this is one of the crosses that selectors have to bear really. It's a very difficult job.

Basically, you are looking at the preparation for a Test match, which of course should be played in the best possible conditions. But you go to a county wicket and the ball may be swinging or spinning or something, quite different conditions from a Test match. And this is one of the things that I feel strongly about, that we've got to get more matches in preparation for Test games. We mustn't forget the three-day and perhaps four-day cricket. Test standard at the moment in comparison with other countries is disappointing because there are so many other pulls on the players with this one-day cricket, and I know particularly from our side that on a Sunday you have to bowl in a certain way and on a Monday in a three-day match you've got to play in quite a different way. I never had this as you know, and it must be very difficult for them, very difficult indeed, but we mustn't lose the Test matches, the showpiece of cricket. And we've got to prepare people for this more, I believe.

Martin-Jenkins: Can we come back to captaincy, and your time as captain? Did you enjoy captaining that successful Surrey side more than the England side, or what were the differences between captaining the two?

May: I enjoyed doing it. As I say we had a good side. I took over from Stuart as you remember, Stuart Surridge who had captained successfully for five years. It was the same people. And I suppose 1957 was probably one of our best years ever, certainly with the Surrey side, and I don't think the responsibility ever worried me because I think, if one's got confidence in the team, it is a team effort and you are only as good as the team plays, aren't you?

I remember walking out to bat at Edgbaston in the famous match with Colin [*Cowdrey*] when we were in the pan. We were struggling, Ramadhin had bowled us out, and as I walked out in the second innings and looked at the scoreboard, we were so far behind it was ridiculous [*61 for 2, 227 runs behind*]. And I remember thinking to myself, well you can only do your best and just go out there and play. And, of course, we had that marvellous partnership, Colin and I, and I remember getting fairly tense at one stage, we'd got quite a few and I was dying to hit Ramadhin straight into Edgbaston High street and charged down the wicket and was nearly stumped, and Colin came and said, 'Now come on, we've got another two days to go yet,' and that sort of thing was marvellous. We got out of the match, and of course won the series. [*They put on 411 for the fourth wicket, May scoring 285 not out and Cowdrey 154.*]

Martin-Jenkins: Yes. And was that your general philosophy of batting, would you say, that you tried to treat each ball on its merits almost?

May: I think the best innings I felt I played was when I went out and tried to relax and just play. I think it's a very difficult thing to do, but I think the more tense one is when one goes out, the less well one tends to play. I think you've got to be relaxed but you've got to move quickly. The worst time of an innings is the first two or three overs when anybody is vulnerable really, and I always said to myself, well, try and move your feet quickly, move the feet. But at the same time it was nice to get off the mark.

Martin-Jenkins: But were you conscious of trying to take the initiative from bowlers? Ever? Were you ever thinking, well, if I don't hit soon he's going to spin such a web round me that I never will?

May: I think it's very important, when one walks out to bat, that one tries to announce one's presence. When one was in the field and one saw a new batsman coming in, one got an impression of somebody, how they came out to bat, whether they were looking neat, whether they looked determined. I mean, there are some batsmen today who play for England, who walk out as though they are rather apologetic about walking out, and don't look as though they're really meaning business. I think probably today that one doesn't see enough conscious effort by either the bowler or the batsman to take charge and say right, this is my day, come on!

Martin-Jenkins: You could hardly accuse someone like Fred Trueman, in your day, of that sort of approach, or today of someone like Dennis Lillee. If you'd been facing Lillee with his rather bombastic attitude, you know he's always there and he's always going to take charge, how would you try to deal with him?

May: He's a very good bowler, of course he is. I never played against him, so I wouldn't like to say that he's a better bowler than Ray Lindwall, for

117

example, or Keith Miller when he was really going. He's a very fine bowler, but he can only bowl one ball at a time. It would be a battle. But again one comes back to the conditions, and I think if it was a slow wicket, one would get the feeling that he was only going to be able to be really attacking for so long. And one would have to sum the whole thing up and see how he was bowling. It's very difficult to sort of generalise, but I think if one tends to get cramped against a bowler like that, it gives him quite a lot of encouragement.

Martin-Jenkins: Who were the bowlers you most respected, of all the ones you played against?

May: I suppose Ray Lindwall on all conditions was the greatest bowler I played, and that's excluding anybody from England. He bowled me that famous over at the Oval, the first time I played against him, in 1953, when I was playing for Surrey in my first match against them. It was a grey May morning, and Ray was swinging the ball, really moving it beautifully. And I was in fairly quickly, and he bowled me four away-swingers, which I played at and missed, and then one in-swinger, which I played at and missed, and the last one I think I made contact with. And I thought to myself, well, I don't know, I shall be quite glad to get out if it's as difficult as this. And in fact I think someone the other end got me out, and I thought this is going to be quite a problem. He is a fine bowler. And I remember some years later, he had a deep mid-off and an extra cover, fairly deep, at Melbourne when I was batting, which I felt was evening things up a little bit.

*   *   *

Colin Cowdrey

Cricket – A Way of Life, April 1976
Colin Cowdrey: I suppose my family were nuts on the game. My father must have been crackers to call me MCC, and from a very early age I was playing it in the garden. I wouldn't have thought I was any different to anyone else in that way, except I did just happen to love the game of cricket and I enjoyed reading about it, and I swotted up my Wisden, I knew all the players' names, but of course I had the disadvantage of no television, so I didn't know any of them by picture. That's where the chaps are so lucky today, aren't they?

Christopher Martin-Jenkins: On the other hand, do you think possibly it takes some of the magic experience out of it, for a young boy going actually to watch a cricket match for the first time?

Cowdrey: I think that's a very good point. It was still magic for me when I started playing for Kent. I'd just been to Tunbridge Wells to watch Kent one afternoon, but the players, I had never met them and they hadn't coached me in the school holidays or anything like that.

Martin-Jenkins: Of the various landmarks you achieved, is it possible now to look back and say which was the most exciting for you?

Cowdrey: Playing at Lord's for the first time as a Tonbridge schoolboy. I was so ill with nerves that morning, walking to the ground and peering at the W. G. Grace gates and entering the Pavilion and walking through the Long Room. But perhaps more significantly was to hear my name in the seventeen to go to Australia, in 1954, that took a lot of believing. Then to get out to Australia and you are playing with Hutton and Compton, and possibly to find myself batting with these maestros. I remember batting with Len Hutton for the first time at Perth, I had to keep touching my arm, pinching myself, you know. I wondered whether this was true. I couldn't take my eyes off him, because he didn't call a great deal then, he sort of ran by instinct, and I was much more concerned whether I ran him out than to earn my own knock.

Martin-Jenkins: Did he put you at ease, was he good at doing that?

Cowdrey: We came to know each other very well and we became huge friends, father and friend to me actually, but it took a little time to build a relationship.

Martin-Jenkins: Would you put him at the top of the list of the captains you played under?

Cowdrey: Oh certainly, yes. I think like all the captains he would be vulnerable to criticism. But who isn't? I mean, we'd all like to be pretty free of criticism, I suppose, but there are not many captains over the years whom you couldn't get at, and Len was vulnerable on a number of counts. But he was steeped in cricket and he had a great touch and he had a great presence.

Martin-Jenkins: Len Hutton of course was succeeded really by Peter May as England captain, and he and Peter are very much part of an era of English batsmanship. Do you look upon your relationship with Peter as a valued one?

Cowdrey: Oh yes indeed. He was my closest friend in cricket. We shared a cabin on my first tour to Australia and then I was vice-captain to him in Australia, 1958/9, and again I was vice-captain to him in West Indies and in England. We travelled together everywhere. I was usually his chauffeur at all the home Test matches. Apart from having a terrific admiration for him as a person, as a batsman he was supreme. He was a truly great player, there was no doubt about that – dominant, powerful, pretty good brain. Complete cricketer, complete batsman.

I say that with one reservation. If he were to get out at all in the latter stages, it was a short-pitched ball because he rather eschewed the hook, and probably in the first ten years of my career we didn't get posed this problem to the extremes that we're posed now. And clearly if Peter had started say in 1960, he would have got down to it and released his answer. But this was the only weakness I ever saw in his batting. But the memory of batting with him, of course, is etched upon our partnership against the West Indies. We batted together for part of Saturday evening, all Monday, until after lunch Tuesday. So it was quite something!

Martin-Jenkins: Did you enjoy being captain more than not being captain, or vice versa?

Cowdrey: I loved it, yes. I loved captaining Kent, which I did for, what, fifteen years. Had the fun of building something and seeing us eventually win things and create a side round one, and a lot of good players come through, like Derek Underwood and Alan Knott, Brian Luckhurst, Mike Denness, Bob Woolmer. If you're talking about England captaincy, that's something I would like to have done more of. I am sure a number of people would say the same. Ray Illingworth, I am quite certain, would say that he got better at it. Once he was in the seat of the England captaincy, the more assured and more comfortable and better captain he became. I captained about twenty-five Tests in all, at various stages. It was just unfortunate that just as Alec Bedser telephoned me to invite me to captain all six Test matches at home [*1969*], which is something that had never been done before, I pulled my Achilles tendon literally an hour later, and that finished my career as far as the England captaincy was concerned.

Martin-Jenkins: Was that the number one regret of all?

Cowdrey: Yes, a disappointment I suppose. It would have been nice to have ended up taking a side, the England side that one had built, to Australia and won the Ashes. That might have been a complete picture for me. But, you know, if I had to look at it in the light of playing twenty-five years of first-class cricket, which I have – and I've played so long in the Test match scene – I've got to be so grateful to remain fit. Very few people remained as fit as I have over that time. Take a chap like Denis Compton, who was cruelly knocked by his knee, you know. You could go through a whole host of players who had a lot of fun but only for half a career. I'm very lucky that I had a tremendous time of it.

Martin-Jenkins: So far as I know the only consistent criticism that has ever been made against your batting was that sometimes you were too introspective about it – that you didn't let your own natural ability have full play. Is there something in that, do you think?

Cowdrey: You know, I am not sure I am the best judge of that really. Not being introspective I'm not sure that . . . ! No, I know what my critics mean, and obviously if one could have one's time again you feel you could play it all so much better. But that's life. We can only have one shot. We can't go back again.

Martin-Jenkins: Looking on the brighter side, which innings gave you the greatest satisfaction?

Cowdrey: Well, I suppose my first hundred for England in 1954 against Australia at Melbourne, when we were in the cart. I think we were 40 odd for four, we ended up only about 190. You know, to get a hundred out of that – it was a clean hundred, I don't think I was dropped. It was one of those days when everything went right, and yet in the middle of it I had forty minutes stuck on 64. Whether this is one of your moments of introspection I don't know, but they pushed the field round and tried to peg me away from the bowling, which they did very successfully for three or four overs, but I got off 64 and I swept to 100 before anyone could look round. And that was a day to remember. And then, of course, last year I had the great fun of taking Kent to an unexpected victory [*against Australia*] at Canterbury. On the last day we were left with about 360 or something, and my 150 there gave me a lot of pleasure, especially when Ian Chappell had called for the bus at 3 o'clock in the afternoon!

Martin-Jenkins: What are the plans for the future?

Cowdrey: Obviously I shall stick very close to the game I love, in the years to come. The game has really never been so healthy in so many ways. There is more interest in it, it's more read, it's more listened to on radio, it's more watched on television, all over the world. I am sure the game is healthier now than when I came into it. And all, I think, that we have to guard really is the balance of money and the true sportsmanship. That may sound slightly trite but I think it's true. There is less real authoritative leadership on the field and that puts an extra strain on authority. I've always felt that the game is always happiest and best when the players run themselves and the captain is really in charge of it all. And that the game has always been weakest when the players have rather stood aside and said let them get on with it, it's up to them, they made the decisions, they, they, they, and that's how the game becomes weak. It's our game, the players' game, and the game will be strong again I think if the leaders, the captains of the game, actually really get involved.

*   *   *

Richie Benaud

Radio 2, July 1963

Rex Alston: Richie, the last time I saw you bowl in England was at the Oval in 1961. Well, there was nothing particularly memorable about that as far as I can remember, but what I do remember, of course, was that wonderful match at Old Trafford, two or three weeks beforehand.

Richie Benaud: Yes, I think probably the Manchester match will be the one that sticks in my memory more than any other game I've ever played. It was a wonderful cricket match apart from being a great finish from the Australian point of view, and it came at a time when we had various injuries and various setbacks in the tour, and it couldn't, I suppose, have come at a better time. There's a lot been talked about the tied Test match in Brisbane with the West Indies in 1960/61, but I think probably the Manchester game was the best game of cricket I've ever known. A tied Test match couldn't be anything else but a wonderful finish, but this Manchester game had fluctuation right through, from the time the first ball was bowled on the first morning. They got us out in the first innings, they then got ahead of us when they batted, May played very well, and all of the batsmen combined to give them a good lead. And then we had Lawry and Simpson who came in and opened the innings for us and gave us a good start and our later batsmen did well, and it wasn't until the last morning of the game that we really got into terrible strife when we had the three wickets, Mackay and myself and Wally Grout, for no runs, to young David Allen. And then, of course, we had that wonderful partnership between McKenzie, the young 19-year-old who had been taken over for experimental purposes really, and Davidson, the veteran all-rounder, probably, I think, with Miller able to rank in the first two or three all-rounders that we've ever had. These two players, the old and the young, put on this wonderful partnership of 98 runs and gave the bowlers the chance later on to try for a victory. In the first instance the victory seemed to be a long way away, because Dexter was attempting to tear our bowling to little pieces – and he did so, he played this wonderful short innings of 76. Then in the end, when the luck ran a little bit our way, we had some great catching, wonderful fielding and out-cricket by our chaps [*and Benaud himself took 6 for 70*], and the pendulum swung a little. It was a memorable game. The thing that makes me very sorry is not taking part in another Test match against England.

Alston: Why are you going to retire, when you are really still such a young man?

Benaud: I think the first thing to say is that I've played sixty Test matches in the years that I've been representing Australia. I think probably that that's enough Test matches for anyone. Once you get up over the fifty or sixty mark, it's a lot of games accrued against other countries. That's one thing. I've got a family and I've got a job, I've got a career that I want to try and map out for myself. I think all in all I've had a pretty good run. Also, there are plenty of other young fellows in Australia and in Australia we bring on the young chaps much quicker than you do over here. Our 18-year-olds in Australia might well be playing for their country. Your 18-year-olds over here are probably still at school, or perhaps making a name for themselves in university cricket, but they never quite capture the public imagination at that age. In Australia we're talking now about a young chap called [*Ian*] Chappell in South Australia, and Chappell is a very good player, he's had in the last two years some very fine performances, and I feel probably that he'll develop eventually into an Australian cricketer. But the point is that out there we talk about him now as an Australian cricketer.

Alston: Do you get bored with the strain of big cricket after all these Test matches?

Benaud: No, I don't think you ever get bored. You never get bored with playing cricket for a start. I think sometimes village matches can be more entertaining for the players than Test matches. Test matches can be a big strain, they can create a bit of a mental hazard at times. No, that's not the reason I'm giving it up; I rather like the strain of Test cricket, if anything. It's a question of knowing when you are just about at your top or just a little bit past it and then retiring from the game. I don't want to go out of the game when I'm well past it, and when I retire I am going to go and play club cricket in Australia. And I'll play that probably for fifteen and twenty years, until I can hardly move on the cricket field. The joints and the bones get very stiff and sore on a Saturday afternoon. But basically it's because I think the time has come to retire, and I think when you decide that then you should do it.

Alston: I'm sure you're right there. And talking about playing club cricket, what about your early life? Were you born into a cricketing family?

Benaud: Yes, I suppose so. My great-grandfather was French. He came from a place called La Rochelle, which is somewhere on the coast of France, I think, a place that I very much want to see this year. And my grandfather wasn't terribly interested in cricket although he encouraged my father. My father was a good cricketer and he played for the same club that I play for in Sydney at the moment, a club called Central Cumberland, which has English leanings – the name came from Cumberland over here – and it's been in existence for upwards of 100 years now. Well, my father played there from 1937 to 1956, for nineteen years, and he's taken the fourth highest number of wickets in the club. He's a very good country cricketer; he played against the New South Wales team that came into the country, and I think from memory that he knocked over Kippax and two or three of the other State players in the game he played and he made 70 or 80 runs as well.

Alston: What sort of stuff did he bowl?

Benaud: He bowled leg-spinners and he was a good one. I played with him in club cricket. It was the first father and son combination in Sydney club cricket. In fact, to begin with I played with him and then I displaced him from the team, which wasn't quite so funny! And he played second grade for some years and then he went down to thirds and then he retired.

Alston: Did he actually coach you in this, or did you simply follow father's example?

Benaud: Well, everything I know about leg-spin bowling I learned from my father. We used to bowl in the backyard and on the back lawn, and I used to go down to the club practices of a weekday, Tuesday and Thursday, and I used to work very hard and he used to encourage me and I used to field for the first grade players when they were in the nets, I used to be out on the fence, used to be a great thing on a Thursday afternoon to try not to let any balls get through for four or to hit the boundary behind me.

Alston: What were your pet subjects at school, if you had any?

Benaud: Well, I didn't really have any. I liked English very much and I rather enjoyed doing essays and compositions when I was in the lower school. I think if there was anything else I liked it was probably chemistry, and at one stage I had some thought of going on and doing something with chemistry, perhaps teaching, and I rather enjoyed doing mathematics, but basically I enjoyed doing English and I think that may have been a help to me in my journalistic career.

Alston: Didn't you say that your father was a schoolmaster?

Benaud: Yes, he was for years a schoolmaster in country areas, where he was the only teacher at the school. In fact that was where – let's see, 1937, what's that, twenty-six years ago? – that was where I heard the Australia/England series, the 1936/37 series, the team of which 'Gubby' Allen was skipper. And I heard that and then the 1938 series, when Bradman brought the team across here, on a little wireless in the town of Jugiong in Australia. Jugiong is about four or five hundred miles from Sydney and it used to be very much in the outback, just on the banks of the Murrumbidgee River. Now it's a much more go-ahead town, there are some thousands of people there, but in those days it was rather a remote area. I used to play cricket on my own, because I was the only boy within two miles of the school, and we had a store-room there with four concrete walls and I used to throw a tennis ball up against one of the walls, and when it came back I'd hit it. And at different time of the day I was Hutton or Bradman or Robinson who played for Australia a few times, or Worthington or Fagg, any of these chaps at any time of the day.

Alston: Well then, when you left school what was your first job?

Benaud: I went straight to an accountant's office for a couple of years, and then I went to the newspaper for which I now work. And I worked in the accounts section there for quite a few years, and then I transferred across to the editorial and for seven or eight years I've been on the editorial staff as a full-time journalist.

Alston: But you are not specifically a cricket reporter, are you? You're an all-purpose chap?

Benaud: Yes, I went on to the editorial side in the first instance as a police roundsman which is the same as a crime reporter over here. And that was the first part of the job, and then I went on to general. I've never actually done sport. I do a sporting column once a week and I do some special sporting feature articles, but I've never actually done sports reporting. I have spent some time on the subs table before the last MCC tour of Australia but I'm afraid the Chief Sub didn't see a great deal of me because of the interference from cricket.

Alston: What did you think of England when you first got here, Richie, in 1953, ten years ago?

Benaud: Well, it should be sufficient to say that I keep on coming back each year. I am back again here this year and I was here in 1961 and I came across to do the South African tour in 1960 and I was here as a player in 1956 and 1953. I came across with Lindsay Hassett the first time, in 1953, and that was a memorable tour because there were so many great names in the side. Miller and Lindwall, and Hassett himself who was a wonderful character and a great captain, and then we had Bill Johnston and Doug Ring, all of them characters in their own way, and it was a wonderful grounding for a young player on his first time away from home. I liked England at first sight, when we came into Tilbury; it was one of those grey mornings that you so often strike early in April in England, it still looked attractive, and when we got up to London I can still remember walking up Piccadilly in the middle of the day, going up towards the Circus itself, and saying, well, this is one of the prettiest things I've ever seen. And I've thought that ever since. I like the country, I like to get away from London, although I love London a great deal, I like to get away out in the country and drive through a few of those quite famous leafy lanes and stay at one or two of the outback, if I might use the Australian term, some of the outback English hotels. This to me is what goes to make up an enjoyable English summer.

Alston: Did you find it very difficult to adapt yourself, cricket-wise, when you came here first?

Benaud: I did. I found the first tour very difficult indeed. I'd like to come back again in 1964, if only for the reason I think I could make 1000 runs. I wouldn't care much about taking 50 or 100 wickets but I'd like to come back and make 1000 runs because I've never done it.

Alston: You think you know how to cope with our wickets now, after all these years?

Benaud: Yes. As a matter of fact I'm looking forward to batting in Australia this year. It's one of those things, I've been a bowler for years, although I started out as a batsman, and I'm looking forward to getting back to the batting now, to be able to bat for a club or bat for New South Wales. But the conditions here are quite different from Australia. Everyone knows that as a basic fact, but how to overcome them is another matter, and it's a question mainly of trying to play exactly as you do in Australia but playing a little later, making sure there's no gap between bat and pad, concentrating all the time and watching the ball terribly closely. If you relax for a moment and don't watch the ball, it's liable to move off the seam, or swing in the air, just do something that it would have no chance at all of doing in Australia. Sometimes in Australia you can play almost blindly down the wicket and hit the ball.

Alston: And as to bowling, well you've got to pitch it up just that little bit further?

Benaud: You must pitch it up quite a bit more, yes. You can't possibly be short over here, particularly early in the season when the wickets are damp. You've got this rather soft 'plasticiney' type of wicket, that the ball hits and stops. It digs in and it's impossible to expect to keep the batsman quiet or get him out unless you keep the ball up. You've got to make him drive, you can't let him pull at all. He must be made to come forward and drive all the time.

Alston: Well, now you've played in every first-class cricketing country, I suppose?

Benaud: Yes. The West Indies is a wonderful place, I'd love to go back there. Perhaps not as a player because, when I get there possibly as a writer in 1965, Wes Hall and Griffith will just about be at their peak I should think, and I don't know that I'd care very much to go out and face them at the age of thirty-five on one of the quick Kingston wickets, but I'd love to go as a writer. We had a wonderful time there in 1955.

Alston: Anything you remember especially about it? Apart from the fact that you won.

Benaud: Well, we won 3–0, but the cricket was quite out of this world.

Although two of the Tests we won quite easily, some of the run-getting performances were quite fabulous. Walcott was the man who stood out and just kept on hitting hundreds off us. It was a wonderful tour. [*Walcott hit five centuries, including a hundred in each innings twice, and scored 827 runs in the series. For Australia Harvey and Miller both hit three centuries, Harvey averaging over 100. In the final Test Benaud made 121, his century coming in only 78 minutes, then the third-fastest ever in Tests.*]

Alston: Coming back to yourself, Richie, when you were at school did you have any opportunities of trying yourself out as a leader?

Benaud: I was captain of the cricket team at school, fourth grade and then first grade, but it's quite a different thing to captaining a major side. I captained my club later on for a little while, and then I captained the New South Wales side once when Miller had to drop out with a bad back, he couldn't play against Victoria in the centenary match. But that was a very brief introduction to any form of leadership.

Alston: You were suddenly pitchforked into this Test cricket, without a great deal of training, as for instance one would have in this country where you would probably be a county captain.

Benaud: Yes, well it was 1955 when I led the side when Miller was hurt. Then in 1956 Ian Craig was captain of New South Wales, and it wasn't until 1958 that suddenly I was made captain, and it was quite a surprise actually.

Alston: Did you find straight away that captaincy affected your cricket?

Benaud: I enjoyed it and I found it a challenge, a great challenge, in the sense that you had not only yourself to think about but you had to think about the other ten fellows in the team, even the twelfth man – you had to worry about what his worries were. And it was a challenge in that sense, and also that you had another team to beat. Now when you are a player you try and beat the other side, you try and beat the chap you are bowling against or batting against at that particular moment, but it doesn't really mean all that much to you when you are captain, and you know you've got to try and weld the side together and you've got to lead them to victory if possible, or draw if not possible. If you lead them to defeat then things are not so good.

Alston: Are you the sort of chap that does a great deal of thinking about this off the field, or do you act on inspiration and intuition?

Benaud: I stop thinking at about 6 o'clock every night, I start again at about 11.30 the next morning! I think there's far too much theory goes into captaining a side and I don't think you can do anything by theory except know what a batsman's weaknesses may be. There's a tremendous amount of theory goes into the game these days. I must say that I don't believe in it,

I think that when you play between 11.30 and 6.30 you play as hard and as well as you possibly can. You do everything that's possible to bring victory to your side, and at the same time to do well yourself. Now once 6.30 comes, then you stop, and you go and have a quiet drink with the other side, and you go out and you enjoy yourself, and at 11 o'clock the next morning the game's on again. I think that's the only way to play the game, and theory doesn't matter two hoots.

Alston: Did you find any difference in captaining sides against England on the one side and, shall we say, the West Indies on the other?

Benaud: Well, there's a difference of course between English players and West Indian players. There's also a difference between West Indian players and Australian players. Now, I think the West Indians are the most exciting players in the world. I don't think Australians are as exciting players as, let's say, Kanhai and Sobers and these chaps. A good example is just to take one stroke. If O'Neill plays a straight drive he can hit it as well as any West Indian that's ever been born. If he plays a sweep he will play it standing up, perhaps half-crouching and bending his knee, and hits the ball in the middle or it hits the fence and bounces back 15 or 20 yards and it's four runs. Now if Kanhai or Sobers do the same thing they are just as likely to fall over, and there's a roar from the crowd, and this is an exciting shot. This is what we found in Australia. That these players, they didn't outscore us by much in a series, they scored 40-something runs for 100 balls and we did the same thing. We bowled more overs, I think, than they did, and by and large we used to get through our overs quite a bit quicker, because they had Wes Hall and often they had Chester Watson playing. And we bowled in the main at the stumps, occasionally used to bowl round about leg stump, but the cricket was exciting. Now I'd go ten miles to watch a West Indian player bat. I mightn't go a hundred yards to watch an Australian or an Englishman – I probably would, because I like cricket, but this is the balance. That these fellows are exciting players, and even more exciting players than we are or than your players are.

Alston: Who's the best captain that you've played under?

Benaud: If you were to take everything into account, probably Miller.

Alston: I always felt that. I always wished he'd captained a side here. I think we should have had a wonderful tour.

Benaud: Well, I think Miller is a wonderful cricketer. It's difficult to say who was the best cricketer we've ever had, but in my time he and Davidson would be the two finest all-rounders that I've ever known. Miller was quite an inspiring captain for New South Wales. When I first came on the scene there Arthur Morris was captain, and I've got a tremendous amount of time for Arthur, he's a great chap and he was a very good captain in a quiet sort of way. Miller was more flamboyant as you well know, and I think that I learnt more technically from Miller than from any other captain.

Alston: But he doesn't give that impression, does he?

Benaud: He gives the impression that he doesn't care a great deal. In fact he never misses a trick, he never misses a thing that's going on. Hassett was a good captain. He was quiet and he never missed a trick either, and he had the disadvantage on that tour of having a pretty good side without having a great side, and he also had three or four young players who were nowhere near as good as they were to be later on. There were Davidson and Archer and de Courcy and myself, and Archer and Davidson and myself later on did quite well for Australia but at that time we were burdens on Hassett because we weren't batting very well and we weren't bowling very well. Archer on occasions bowled well, and so did Davidson till he got hurt, but there were a couple of times when I had the responsibility of trying to bowl sides out and I just couldn't do it because I wasn't a very good bowler. And a couple of times I failed with the bat when I should have made runs, and this is the thing that happens to all young players. Hassett wasn't deterred by this, and used to give us all the encouragement around the world, and this was a great thing to us. I think that he was a very good skipper. They are the two best, I think, but Miller would shade any of them as far as I'm concerned.

Alston: Now what about the best captain that you've played against?

Benaud: Difficult, that. The first one was Hutton of course, in 1953. I wouldn't say that Len was a great captain, he was a thinker and a worrier. I would think that May was the best captain I've –

Alston: Had to compete against.

Benaud: Yes. I would think so. He was a bit unlucky in 1958/59, he got very bad press, and he had a side that was just a bit over the hill and we knew this before they arrived in Australia and we capitalised on it. I think Peter was unfortunate there. He got a bad press through no fault of his own, and at times he got a vicious press, which is even worse.

Alston: As a result he's no longer playing cricket, and I think that that's probably the reason.

Benaud: Well, that could well be. I think myself it's a tragedy. Worrell is a fine captain. He's a fine captain in the sense that every player in his side has a tremendous amount of time for him. Anything Frank says to any of the chaps on this tour, or in Australia in 1960/61, would be done just like that. No trouble at all. May I think of as a very hard and very fair captain, who was unlucky and unfortunate. Worrell I think of as a gay captain, who did so much for our cricket in Australia. It's an entirely different type of comparison.

Alston: Looking to the future, Richie, what do you want to do?

Benaud: Well, there are a lot of things I could do, Rex, but I think most of all I want to be able to play club cricket against Sydney, every Saturday afternoon. I could go and become a writer of sorts or a journalist of sorts, and I want to work at that very hard and cover both those angles, but the thing I want to do is to play for my club, Cumberland. I started off with them and I want to go back to them after this next couple of years are over, and I want to play Saturday afternoon cricket. It's quite a different method of playing. I pay five shillings every Saturday afternoon for the privilege of playing cricket for my club, which rather amuses me when I hear some talk of the amateur/professional status over here. But if I can play perhaps for the next fifteen years at five shillings a time every Saturday afternoon, my cricket career will be quite happy. I'd like to become a good writer, I'd like to be a good cricket journalist, but I think the thing I'd like most of all is to be able to get back to the Cumberland Club where I started, play my cricket. We've got a very young side there, average age of about eighteen or nineteen, and that is the thing that I'd like to do, to bring those young chaps on, and to play with them, and to just put back a little bit into the game that I've taken out of it over the twelve or fourteen years.

*　　*　　*

Dennis Lillee

Wogan's World, July 1975
Terry Wogan: Dennis, during last season's Test series against Australia you were pictured by the British press, at least, as a 'bit of a villain' – shouting and swearing at the batsmen –

Dennis Lillee: It's all true.

Wogan: But you're going to say you're not really like that, aren't you?

Lillee: Well, I did do it!

Wogan: What inspired you? Were the batsmen infuriating you or is that you on the field?

Lillee: Well, I play it very hard on the field. I always have done. I don't like batsmen getting runs against me. If they do I get upset and it helps my game. That's my only excuse.

Wogan: Are the qualities of aggression and hostility necessary to be a great fast bowler?

Lillee: No.

Wogan: What's the quality you need?

Lillee: I don't know. If ever I do reach it I'll let you know.

Wogan: To succeed in any sport d'you think one needs to have a killer instinct?

Lillee: Yes, I think to succeed in most things you must have a sort of killer instinct, or perhaps a will to win.

Wogan: Well, for somebody like me who is pretty well untutored in cricket, the controversy was about bouncers. How do you feel about the bouncer?

Lillee: It's a legitimate weapon for a fast bowler and I've bowled it for a long time and I'll keep bowling it. I don't think it should be used at tail-end batsmen, but the circumstances were such that it was used in Australia against tail-end batsmen and it was unfortunate. I hope it doesn't happen again.

Wogan: Is that part of the freemasonry of fast bowlers, that they don't bowl fast at each other? When you say tail-end batsmen that's usually the fast bowler, isn't it?

Lillee: A lot of time it is, although most of them think they can bat! I think a tail-end batsman, unless he makes a lot of runs – by a lot, I mean 20 or 30 runs – shouldn't expect a bouncer. But if he does make a few runs, he's been hanging around for a while, he's become a batsman in my opinion and he should expect a bouncer.

I'll tell you an interesting story about bouncers. I was out of cricket because of my back and I decided to play as a batsman in club cricket. I'd been giving these club cricketers hell over the five or six years before, and here's me playing as a batsman only, and you can imagine the number of bouncers I got during that season thinking that I wouldn't be bowling again. But I've got the names in a black book and I'll remember next time I'm playing against them!

Wogan: Well now, a lot of commentators here are decrying the apparent decline of what they call the gentlemanly qualities that one always associated with cricket. Do you think it's becoming a more violent game?

Lillee: I really don't. Look, Australians play it hard, South Africans play it hard, the English play it hard. Everyone plays it hard when they play cricket, but our style of game has moved with the generation. A lot more people swear now, whether you like it or not, it's an outlet of frustration at not getting a wicket or being hit around. As far as I'm concerned it doesn't mean that it's not a gentlemanly game any more. I just think, as things have changed in the world, so has cricket.

Wogan: Look how violent soccer crowds have become here – because, they say, of the increased violence on the pitch one leads to the other. Do you think cricket crowds will become increasingly unruly as the players on the field become more unruly?

Lillee: I think soccer is a bit different because a crowd sometimes has to wait for forty-five, fifty or seventy minutes before something happens. And when that happens they've built themselves up so much that something's liable to happen in the crowd. But in cricket there's something happening all the time, so the release is in small forms. So I don't think it'll ever get to a soccer crowd-type atmosphere.

Wogan: I must be a bit of a philistine because I don't think anything's happening in cricket at all!

Lillee: You've been watching too many Test matches, Terry.

Wogan: You've had a certain amount of injury. Are fast bowlers prone to it, from the way they hurl themselves around?

Lillee: Well, they must be. I think one doctor said to me that fast bowling was the most unnatural action in the world and I tend to agree with him. I'm not the only one, everyone has them. In my case, with the back it was stress fractures of the spine. Well, that was a bit hard to overcome just like that, so I had to have a rest and build up again. I would say most fast bowlers at some stage during a season will carry an injury.

Wogan: If injury put you out of cricket, would it be the end of the world for you?

Lillee: No, not at all. It wouldn't worry me at all.

*   *   *

Viv Richards

Radio 4, August 1983

Viv Richards: They knew that I loved playing sport and I loved taking part in cricket and soccer and all that, and if I didn't really get my things done at home, or my homework, they used to hide my trousers. I find it quite funny now. You can be so sports mad at that time and there's no way that I would ever venture out without a pair of pants on or anything like that, and you know, I did my homework. So I could play and wear my trousers as well.

I've got a younger brother by the name of Mervyn, and we used to play quite a lot. I used to represent myself as West Indies and I think he used to be

England. We had five-yard boundaries and things like that. Certainly we had some good times in those days, and certainly I started from an early age. I was in school then, playing school cricket and playing first division cricket. At that time I used to be an off-spin bowler, but maybe because I was the smallest in the team they never seemed to recognise my batting, I was probably just there to make up numbers.

Ted Harrison: Isaac Vivian Alexander Richards, or Viv for short, is now a batsman of prodigious talent. He bats with glorious incaution, with heart-stopping elegance, and at thirty-one must be judged the greatest natural batsman in the world. To watch him at close quarters at the nets last Saturday was to watch a master at work. Although he has many great scores behind him, he's not an accumulator of runs – it has been said of him that he flirts with the record books when he could monopolise them. From an early age he was acknowledged as a cricketer of rare ability. He was sent for six weeks' coaching to London with his fellow islander, the fast bowler Andy Roberts. But it was with the arrival on Antigua of a certain ruddy-faced bookmaker from Bath that a professional career in cricket became possible. Len Creed, later the Somerset county chairman, had arrived in Antigua on holiday. He had spotted a passing reference to Viv in the magazine *The Cricketer*. Viv told me what happened next as we chatted, watching Somerset batting against Lancashire under an Old Trafford sun.

Richards: The first thing I can remember is a taxi driver coming and saying, 'There's this guy from England and he's the Chairman of Somerset County Cricket Club and he's enquiring about you.' And my head swelled really big, you know – bigger than this ground. He came and we went over to where he was staying and we had a little chat, and he was saying it'd be nice if I could come back at the time. The club didn't know anything about it – Somerset County Cricket Club.

Harrison: Entirely his initiative, was it?

Richards: Yes, it was just his, and everything was done according to Len Creed at the time.

Len Creed: Viv had a sort of commitment although nothing was signed, as I was quick to point out to him, to play for Oldham in the Lancashire League. And I said, 'Well, I don't know anything about that, but being as I don't know whether you can bat, if you're ever good enough to come to play for my team, you will find that playing Lansdown, Bath, is a far nicer part of the country than the north country. We get far more sun like the Caribbean.' So the next day Viv plays, and after he had made about 3 or 4 he was stumped by a yard, but the umpire was told I was watching and he gave him not out, and I thought, well, he looks a useful player to me. What impressed me more than anything perhaps was his astonishing fielding at cover point, whereby in an underhand throw he threw some chap out. I turned immediately to the chap who was on my right, who was travelling with me, he was a member of Somerset Committee, and I said, 'Louis, that chap's coming to Somerset, we're going to have him.'

Harrison: Len Creed took a gamble. He paid for Viv's ticket to England himself, confident that Somerset would recognise the young Antiguan's talent and sign him up. However, Len's plans were almost stymied by Her Majesty's immigration officials at Heathrow who, not surprisingly, thought Viv Richards' tale somewhat improbable.

Creed: Viv was there with his head in his hands and the immigration authority said he must return on the next plane, he hasn't got a work permit. I said, 'Well, in that case I shall have to ring the Home Secretary.' I said, 'Surely this chap can come on a holiday or do something, you know. He can't go back on the next plane.' The outcome of it all was that the head chap of the immigration happened to be born in Somerset and had a tremendous allegiance to cricket, and he came along to me and he said, 'I've checked on your credentials, Mr Creed. All seems to be in order and we will let him in if you put him up for a sort of month's holiday. And I'm sure you will find him a job.' And I said, 'Oh yes, I am sure I will.' Which I did. As assistant groundsman at Lansdown Cricket Club, where his hands were just like those that play a Stradivarius fiddle, he was frightened to touch them.

Harrison: Word spread quickly that the reluctant groundsman was a superb cricketer. He became the despair of many a west country club bowler. Eventually Viv was offered a two-year professional contract with the county team. The captain then was Brian Close, well known for his curt tongue and tough no-nonsense approach with the junior team members. Working at Lansdown or being sworn at by Close, was there ever a moment, I asked Viv, when he wanted to pack it all in and return to the sunshine?

Richards: Yes, there were times when I was living with this guy from Barbados, and there I am in this room trying to get some sleep, and that was the room where these guys actually kept their steel drums. So when they came in say, probably like one and two in the morning, I had to get up because of the noise of the steels. But for some reason, I got the will to go on and said life doesn't begin with a sweet in your mouth. There's a few sour grapes as well.

Harrison: But of course your game had to develop, and I believe Brian Close once said to you, 'You've got enough talent, what about some bloody graft?'

Richards: Yes, Brian Close played a very big part in my career. I have a lot of respect for Brian Close. Whenever he comes around to me and says, 'Well, Viv, I don't think you are doing this right,' I respect every word that he says. I used to hear about Brian Close sticking his chest out to my heroes in the West Indies, Charlie Griffith and Wes Hall and people like that, and if I got a little knock I wouldn't wince, I would just say, 'Well, you know, I don't think Brian would be too pleased if I did.' Some of that has helped to rub off on my cricketing career.

Harrison: That was you though, was it, raw talent and no hard work?

Richards: No hard work. I never used to do any hard work, it used to come so easy. I used to go out and just bat and get a quick 40, and I thought that was it, you see.

Harrison: Viv goes to the crease to conjure up excitement. With his cap set back on his head he tends to saunter between the wickets, appearing deceptively casual. That is until faced with a cricket ball hurtling at 80 miles per hour, when in a mere half-second he can decide on and execute one of his astonishing strokes. Viv Richards has been lucky, he's played Test cricket for one of the strongest Test sides ever and county cricket for one of the best teams Somerset has ever fielded. He had seldom been weighed down by responsibility. He's also played at a time when star cricketers can make substantial sums of money. But he isn't a disinterested mercenary. When I spoke to Alan Gibson of the *The Times* at Lord's recently, he extolled Viv's exceptional loyalty to his adopted county.

Alan Gibson: He became, from quite an early stage of his association, a genuine Somerset man. This has not always been to his advantage. Do you remember that year when Somerset lost two finals in two days – well, not exactly that, but they lost the Gillette on the Saturday and lost the decisive match of the John Player on the Sunday – and Vivian was deeply upset about this. In fact it spoiled his play. He played too carefully on the Saturday and then everyone said, 'No, you must have a swish tomorrow, you mustn't be so stodgy, have a go! Play your strokes.' And Somerset lost both matches and I remember how deeply upset Vivian was. And that was an indication of how much he felt devoted to the Somerset cause.

Richards: That particular weekend just all turned sour, because in over 107 years, or something like that, we hadn't won anything. I can remember I had a very nice bat of mine, a bat that I'd used throughout the season because I'd done pretty well with that bat, and after the last game I smashed it and just broke down in tears because I couldn't believe that players could work so hard and be robbed of everything in that one weekend. But gradually I came through, and we went back the following year and we had our consolation. It wasn't any crying and things like that then. It was just joy and pleasure.

Harrison: And Viv's 117 guaranteed the 1979 Gillette Cup. Viv Richards is strongly tipped to take over from Clive Lloyd as captain of the West Indies, but there must be a question-mark over his temperament. Viv to blame, said the papers, when the West Indies astonishingly lost to India in the World Cup final in June [1983]. Although Viv was the side's highest scorer, he was out for 33 when all set for a match-winning innings. His batting was described as irresponsible. Then there's the incident of the door he smashed at Harrogate when someone in the crowd called him a black bastard. And Viv can never forget the day he caused a riot playing for Antigua when he disputed a lbw decision.

Richards: I showed my disapproval by stamping about a few times, which I shouldn't have done really as a youngster. I was a little bit raw and behaving in a kind of very disorderly manner by shouting abuse at the umpire as well. I behaved really bad, you know, and seeing my disapproval by not walking and behaving in this disorderly fashion, the crowd stormed onto the field and in a matter of minutes they had placards and everything, with No Viv No Match, and they reinstated me and I went back, just in order to keep the crowd happy and still at the time. I just couldn't cope with going in to bat again, because I thought that wasn't cricket, and not knowing where I was and all that, I got out.

Harrison: And he was out again for a duck in the second innings, and has the unique distinction of being out three times for nought in one match. I talked about Viv, the sportsman, with Clive Lloyd in the skipper's dressing-room at Old Trafford.

Clive Lloyd: Like most West Indians he's a very bad loser. I think the only good loser's the person that loses often, and we are not accustomed to losing. That's why I suppose we tend to be a little bit more subdued when we've lost. Because we have really done very well over the last eight or nine years.

Harrison: How does he take it out on himself, though, if he gets out with a silly stroke perhaps, when he's going well?

Lloyd: Oh well, he throws the bat often into a fling, but you can see he's very annoyed. He's uptight for a couple of minutes until it's worn off. That's a true professional. He wants to do well, and he thinks of his personal pride, which is very important.

Harrison: Viv Richards has scored well over 4000 Test runs. He made 291 against England in 1976 on his way to a record [at the time] Test aggregate [in one calendar year]. He heads the first-class averages this year, and holds the record for the most sixes hit in a season of John Player League games. His Test career began in India in 1974/5. He was a surprise choice for the tour and had an unhappy first Test facing Chandrasekhar.

Richards: I used to dread facing this guy. There was I, caught for 3 and 4 off the same guy, you know? I think he's one of the best I've ever faced when it

George Hirst (*top*) does a spot of net coaching in wintry conditions. An aerobatic Gubby Allen (*below*), bowling to Stan McCabe in the 1st Test at Brisbane in 1936 (Jack Fingleton, who made a century, is the non-striker), was one of Hirst's pupils. He took 8 for 107 in the match, which England won

Above: Molly Hyde (*right*), captaining England against Australia at Northampton in the first-ever Women's Test in this country, leads out a sheepish-looking side with Muriel Haddelsey (*centre*)
Below: Six captains of international women's cricket teams line up at the Hurlingham Club before the World Cup competition in 1973. *Left to right:* Yolande Hall (Jamaica), Susan Goatman (Young England), Audrey Disbury (International XI), Miriam Knee (Australia), Bev Brentnall (New Zealand) and Rachael Heyhoe Flint (England)

Sarah Potter in determined mood with ball and bat in the 1987 One-Day International at
Lord's against Australia

Australian skipper Richie Benaud with his Surrey and England counterpart Peter May returning to the pavilion after tossing up before the start of the tourists' game against Surrey at the Oval in 1961. Benaud quietly confident after deciding to bat

For once Dennis Lillee is on the receiving end as Graham Gooch hits out aggressively during the England/Australia one-day match at the Oval in 1980. Geoff Boycott is at the other end and Bill Alley is the umpire

Colin Cowdrey smiles at the thought of what he will do to the women's bowling in a benefit match against the England Women's XI at Sittingbourne

A typically Bothamesque lofted drive over cover

Even the great have to practise. Viv Richards keeps his eye on the ball

Richard Hadlee giving nothing away. Lloyd Budd is the umpire

Barry Richards drives, Rod Marsh watches

Frank Chester signals, Dicky Bird warns. An uncomfortable moment for West Indian captain Rohan Kanhai during the Lord's Test of 1973 after a spate of bouncers from Keith Boyce. Roy Fredericks listens in. West Indies won by an innings and 226 runs, Boyce taking 8 wickets

Top: England's captain David Gower with a champagne shampoo as he raises a replica
of the Ashes at the Oval in 1985
Bottom: The 21-year-old Gower cuts for MCC v. Pakistan at Lord's in May 1978, shortly
before making his England début in the 1st Test. Wasim Bari is the wicket-keeper, Sadiq
Mohammad at slip

comes to spin bowling, because he wasn't all that slow you know. He used to bowl bouncers and things like that because he had such a whippy arm. For some reason he was left out of the second Test, where he had some kind of an injury, and that's when I went on to make 192 [*not out*] at New Delhi, and by going out and scoring that particular 100 it boosted my confidence so high. I had a score to begin with now and it just all started from there.

Gibson: You'd have a quick bowler on and he'd be bowling good-length stuff outside the off stump or on the off stump with an off-side field, and Richards would keep punching him through the covers for four, finding the gaps. So the bowler would think, oh, this is no good, and switch to the leg side, settle a leg-side field, bowl on or outside the leg stump. And Richards would then step away from the leg stump and hit a good-length ball over extra cover for six. Most extraordinary stroke, he just thought this is the way to cope with this problem.

Harrison: Viv Richards' main problems have been off the field. As superstar he was recruited as a Kerry Packer mercenary to play the new-style showbiz game in Australia, and risked the wrath of the establishment. But despite offers, some say of a million dollars, he's refused to play in South Africa. Indeed, he could take on the status of an honorary white and pick up an open cheque to play in the country any time he wants.

Richards: I've been approached but I wouldn't really like to tell you how much I was approached with or anything like that. I go on majority rule really and I have spoken to the white South African, I have spoken to the black South African, I have spoken to the Afrikaaner, and the white South African tells me that things are all right in the country, but the other three or the other four, they are telling me that it's not the same, you know, and most certainly I'm not tempted at this particular moment to go there for any reason at all.

Harrison: Did you have any qualms, though, about taking Kerry Packer's money?

Richards: No, not really, because it was a different thing completely. I don't think we were doing anybody any harm because look at what happened in the end. It all worked out in the end. We didn't do any harm and it was justified.

Harrison: What about playing, though, in the different circumstances, floodlit cricket, a white ball, dressed up in pink and so on?

Richards: I think it helped. I think Kerry Packer did a lot for world cricket, and you can see exactly from the salaries that the players have been paid. Some say that Kerry Packer only harmed the cricketers themselves, but you look and see how it opened a few eyes, and look at what the establishment are doing now – the same ones who were saying we were pansies for dressing up in pink and yellow and all that – the establishment have gone for it now and it's a big money earner. So I think the biggest thing that ever happened to cricket was Kerry Packer.

Harrison: Kerry Packer gave Viv Richards financial security for himself, his wife Miriam and daughter Matara. His playboy days are over, though he admits to good times past when he was a prime target for the groupies on the cricketing circuit. Viv has three passions in life – his family, his cricket and his music.

Lloyd: Oh, he's a music lover, there's no doubt about it. He can't sing but he loves music.

Harrison: What sort of music?

Lloyd: Well, I think he's into reggae and a bit of soul, like most West Indians calypsos, he seem to like a lot of calypsos. And it's part of West Indies heritage more or less and he just likes music. He plays it loud enough anyway, so you know when he's around!

Harrison: In the aftermath of the World Cup defeat [*1983*], Viv Richards talked about going home for good and putting up his feet in the sunshine. But that now seems unlikely, at least for a few years. His batting has hit a new peak of fluency and the captaincy of the West Indies is within his grasp. It's just a cataract slowly developing in one eye which might bring his career to a premature close. And when he retires?

Richards: I want to go back to Antigua. Ever since I came to this country I have learned a lot. We have been doing a lot of community work as such, you know, trying to get to the kids and let them know there is a future out there. Because there is so much talent especially in Antigua and around the other islands, that with just a little bit of smoothening up I think things could get so much better. I think it's helped to keep them off the street a little bit, trying to let them know there is a future out there for you. There's a future out there representing West Indies and that's everyone's dream, and coming from that particular island, it's a sort of inspiration to those kids to go out and say, well, I want to be an Andy, I want to be a Vivvy, and it's a driving force, you know, for them.

*　　　*　　　*

Ian Botham

Radio 2, February 1984
Gerald Williams: When a sportsman's diet becomes the whole nation's concern and the pedlars of gossip grow eager to chronicle his social life, it's a mark that he's graduated to a new plateau of prominence. At twenty-eight Ian Botham is one of those instantly recognisable public people, England cricketer, captain past and possibly future, Scunthorpe United footballer, joker in the pack, centre of controversy. We talked one afternoon over a cup of tea before he left for the current tour of New Zealand.

Just to begin at the beginning, originally as a kid in Yeovil you were a Chelsea football fan. I can't understand how that happened.

Ian Botham: Well, it was funny actually, as a youngster, living down in Somerset. I wasn't actually born there but I lived all my life that I can remember as a youngster there. The nearest side to us was Southampton, and in those days I was more interested in playing than watching, as I think most kids are. And it was just by chance, I just happened to see Chelsea on television, I think as a very young lad, I suppose in the 1960s some time, and took a fancy to them. I think they got beaten if I remember rightly on television. I felt really sorry for them because they looked like a good side, and it started from that, really. The colours I liked as well. Royal blue has always been one of my favourite colours, stupid as that sounds, and that's how it started, Gerald. And then I also took a liking to Rangers up in Scotland because of the similarity in the way they played at the time, and the colour and everything, and ever since those two sides stuck.

Williams: And as a kid, in your bedroom I suppose you had all the pictures?

Botham: Well, the whole room was totally blue –

Williams: Is it right that your mother once made you some curtains that were blue and white?

Botham: Oh, I insisted on it. The rules were that I had to look after my own room. So I said, if I've got to look after it, I'll have it done the way I want. So they agreed in the end, and I had it royal blue and Mother made me some blue and white curtains up and I was a terrible fanatic in the younger days.

Williams: And yet, when you had a chance to become a professional footballer when you would have been – what, fifteenish? – it was the club I support, Crystal Palace, who came after you. How did that happen?

Botham: Well, from what I can gather it started when I was playing youth football and junior county football at about the age of fourteen/fifteen, and they took an interest. Then, to cut a long story short, it ended up with Bert Head talking to my father and trying to persuade me to join the Palace. There were a couple of other clubs interested as well at the time, but Palace took it further than anyone.

Williams: Do you ever regret that you didn't say yes in those days?

Botham: Well, now obviously I can't regret it because I've had such a great life out of cricket. But there are times when I'm at Scunthorpe and that yard of pace is missing that you used to have and you think it's because of cricket, you know – six-plus hours in the day in the field, as opposed to ninety minutes in training with soccer. So I often wonder where I would have got. Because, you know, for a guy that picks up a football perhaps for a couple of months a year I'm not the worst player around, and I often wonder what could have happened. But it's a dream now.

Williams: The popular conception of you from watching you play cricket – Guy the Gorilla – who gave you the name by the way?

Botham: That was my dear friend Geoff Boycott.

Williams: Oh Mr Boycott called you that. Presumably because of this sort of swinging-from-the-trees type cricket you play?

Botham: Yes, and I think possibly because of my whole make-up, character, you know. I've always been regarded as the joker on tour. You're always down in the dressing-room if you've had a bad day and specially in a Test match against Australia or someone. Well, you can go through that period of blackness if you want. That's not my cup of tea. The way I see it is that, all right, we've had a bad day, to hell with it, we know we've done badly, let's go out there tomorrow and do it right, and let's cheer each other up. It's not the end of the world.

Williams: No. But for all for that, though, you do have apparently a bit of a short fuse. Didn't Ian Chappell get a slight nudge from you on one occasion, and dear Henry Blofeld, poor bloke! So I mean, you can . . .

Botham: Yeah, I think it's in the make-up of any sportsman, you can take so much for so long and then it comes to a head. Luckily it doesn't happen too often.

Williams: Are you able to get over those quickly though? I mean, when you gave Henry Blofeld that much-publicised nudge, in an airport in Australia or something like that? Is it all over five minutes later?

Botham: Oh, as far as I'm concerned, yes And, give Henry his due, it was all over as far as he was concerned. And I think that's the way it should be, because you can't go round bearing grudges in this life, you've got to live with each other. Especially as Henry is involved quite a lot obviously with cricket. So it would be a pretty sick situation if I'm not talking to him and he's not talking to me.

Williams: You are very competitive. I think you yourself have said you can't even lose to your boy Liam, your son. Is that right?

Botham: I think most sportsmen are like that, most good sportsmen, because your job's to win. I can accept defeat, obviously I've got to and I've had to many times, but my objective is to win, and I'll do everything within the laws of the game to do it. Apart from with the Australians!

Williams: I'm sure they appreciate that!

Botham: Well, that's the way they play it.

Williams: So here you are then, this sort of schoolboy hero because of your swashbuckling style that's represented in all the sixes that go flying all over the place, and yet apparently you are, for example, a monarchist. Now is that right, you're a great royalist?

Botham: Very much so.

Williams: You met the Queen one day?

Botham: I've met the Queen quite a few times. I've had the privilege to meet her probably half a dozen times now. I'm very proud of the Royal Family, what they represent, and I think they do an extremely good job for this country. And I wouldn't swop their job for all the tea in China as the old saying goes. I had tea with the Queen at Lord's when I was captain and I just found her a very, very pleasant woman.

Williams: And you don't feel constrained that you have to sort of bow and scrape and find the right phrase?

Botham: Well, I am very much a believer in that form of etiquette. And I found her a very warm woman, and a woman that you could talk to as a person – a charming woman.

Williams: Is she a cricket fan, do you think?

Botham: I think she'd have rather been at Ascot! Mind, if I'd been given the choice, I'd have probably rather been at Ascot!

Williams: Yes, I was going to ask you that. To come on to the real heart of you, I just wonder – being highly competitive and being clearly not, if I may say so without wanting to sound fawning, not arrogant in the least – are you aware of your position in the game, as being in some people's view the greatest of today's all-rounders? One thinks of Imran Khan, Kapil Dev, Richard Hadlee, you. You four are somewhere, aren't you?

Botham: They're all very fine cricketers.

Williams: But would you like to be thought of as the best of the all-rounders today?

Botham: Yes.

Williams: Do you think you are?

Botham: Yes, I think so at the moment. I've had a bit of a quiet period for six months, nine months, but I'm back to fighting fitness, and I'm bubbling and wanting to go again.

Williams: When you lost or gave up the England captaincy – which was it, by the way?

Botham: Well, I think I just beat them to the gallows.

Williams: You think they'd have replaced you?

Botham: Oh yes, I'm sure

Williams: But that wasn't why you did it, was it?

Botham: No, no, that doesn't worry me at all. The reason I did it was primarily because at the time I felt that it was unfair to myself, my family and also, very importantly, the team. Because it was on a match-to-match basis, and there is no stability at the top if the captain doesn't know whether he's coming or going, then I think it's very hard for the team underneath him to settle down and play.

Williams: That was what hurt you – the sort of public trial you were undergoing?

Botham: Yeah, I think that any captain in England at that time would have struggled with the side that we had against the West Indies for virtually a year. I think we lost the series 1–0 or something on those lines, and I think the critics before we left for the tour of the West Indies were saying, Oh, it will be 4–0, a whitewash, and all this sort of thing. Which immediately infuriated me because every other country you go to support their side to the hilt, and yet the media in this country seem to support the opposite. They never seem to want to get right behind the side and give them the encouragement I think they deserve.

Williams: Because they feel – we feel, because it's my trade too – that we have to be quite objective and therefore it's not easy on our side of the fence either. But again, just to defend my own kin, you hadn't captained England to any victory at all in, what was it, twelve Tests?

Botham: I did captain them to victory. I captained them to victory in the one-day international against the West Indies.

Williams: Oh yes. And also during that remarkable period when, having given up the captaincy in 1981, almost alone you won the next three Tests for England – and that was said with the greatest respect to Bob Willis – but it was an absolutely golden period of your life. The same cricket writers and commentators who presumably had been needling you by their criticism were the first to revere you, weren't they?

Botham: Well, let me put it this way, Gerald. In this country the media tend to build up a sportsman into this mould that – I don't particularly like the phrase superstar – but that's the phrase they use. And they build you up and when something goes wrong for you, which it's bound to if you're doing it day in day out, you're going to have your bad runs, you've got to have that little bit of luck, and it deserted me for a period of time. And yet the crazy thing was I was scoring runs galore for Somerset and getting wickets galore. And yet when I came to the Test arenas I was getting out and I couldn't get wickets and one thing and another. It was just going against me. And what annoyed me was that the media seemed to have to find an excuse for their protégé if you like.

Williams: We build you up and then when you don't do it every day we have to chip you down again.

Botham: They have to chip you down. And then the part I enjoyed most was, at the end of that summer against the Australians, when I went through that powerful patch, was watching the plaster being replaced and repainted, and I really enjoyed that!

Williams: Were you able to do that with a degree of generosity or did you actually go round and sort of whack one or two of them, not physically but verbally –

Botham: I made a couple of gestures to the press obviously, just to show them my feelings, and I did it again this summer. But in that particular series, after that Test match at Headingley where I got the 140-odd not out I went down to the press room and I said, 'We'll do an interview,' and I walked down with a big towel gagged round me and just waved to them and walked straight out.

Williams: You enjoyed that!

Botham: Yes. My attitude was, you've had it all to say for the two Tests, three Tests, you say it now . . .
  At Headingley, when I went in in the second innings, it looked like a totally lost cause, and I must be honest, I myself had even booked out of the hotel that morning.

Williams: 500 to 1, wasn't it?

Botham: Yeah, 500 to 1, and unfortunately I was batting when the odds

151

were laid, or I'd certainly have had a few quid on that! But it was a lost cause, so to speak, or it certainly seemed a lost cause, and there was no pressure on myself and Graham Dilley and we just went out and played. There were a few heave-ho's that came off the middle of the bat, and Graham Dilley just swung at everything and middled it, and suddenly we were 50 or 60 in front. And then with two or three wickets to fall I thought, if we can get to a hundred on this wicket and have a bit of luck . . . Then that's what happened and Bob [*Willis*] put the icing on the cake with a magnificent piece of bowling the next day.

Williams: You must have a fair degree of pride. Was it very difficult for you after renouncing the captaincy, to have to play under other captains, Brearley, Fletcher, Willis, Gower?

Botham: No.

Williams: Not a bit?

Botham: Not at all.

Williams: I find that quite surprising really. If that had been me I'd have . . .

Botham: No, my pride is to play for England. All right, captaining the side everyone has their views, and Bob will ask me what I think, same as when I was captain I'd ask him or David Gower or anybody. I was open to any suggestion, and it's very much the same with Bob. And I believe that just playing for my country was high enough, and if I could be of any help, whether it be in scoring a hundred or perhaps suggesting a bowling change that gets us a couple of wickets, well I'm there, that's my job.

Williams: You'd like to be England captain again though, wouldn't you?

Botham: Oh yes.

Williams: Do you think you will?

Botham: I don't know, to be honest.

Williams: But it's interesting that David Gower has now been made captain of Leicestershire and you've been made captain of Somerset, so knowing how we work in our business, there's going to be a great build-up of momentum between you and David Gower.

Botham: Well, to be absolutely honest that's going to be the last of my worries. I am sure that whoever it is that's captain, we'll all be happy to play. I'm speaking mostly for myself but I'm more than certain that David Gower's attitude will be the same.

Williams: You say cricket's been very good to you and it obviously has –

financially too. I think Bob Willis has written that you are well on the way to becoming England's first millionaire cricketer. Is that right?

Botham: I wish someone would tell my accountant that!

Williams: But you must be well off now?

Botham: Well, I've made a good living out of it, yeah. But certainly when you see some of the stories in the press about what I'm meant to have earned, it's pie in the sky.

Williams: But might you be a millionaire one day?

Botham: I don't think through cricket, no.

Williams: You were England's first £1000 a week cricketer, so that was an important thing financially. Is it right somebody paid you – better not say who – £10,000 to shave off that beard? I think that's right, isn't it?

Botham: Well, that's just, that's the commercial side of business, you know it was. I think I'll have to try growing it again and see what happens.

Williams: But then you put your name to a newspaper column, you do this marvellous advertisement – which I think is brilliant, whoever dreamed that one up – advertising a form of shoes which has this picture of you, and it says as worn by the Scunthorpe United reserve centre forward. That's another side of your income. There's breakfast cereal and so the money's rolling in. What would you do with it all? I mean, you've got a lovely home up in Lincolnshire.

Botham: My ambition, at the moment, when I finish cricket is to go into breeding horses. That's just a dream at the moment.

Williams: Really? Where did it come from, do you think, this interest in horses? It seems not just to be an interest in horse-racing, much more of the bloodstock.

Botham: Yeah, much more. I am probably getting more and more interested in the bloodstock side of it and in the breeding than I am in the actual racing. Although I enjoy racing obviously because that's the icing on the cake. Well, I'd just like to have a farmhouse with a few stables and a few acres of land to get on quietly with my breeding.

Williams: Where will it be?

Botham: Well, I'm very happy living where I live now, up in north Lincolnshire.

Williams: I can't quite understand why you live there, when you're playing cricket for Somerset.

Botham: Well, there's a couple of reasons really. Because I've worked down in Somerset for most of my career in cricket, it's nice to be able to get away from that environment, because no one likes sleeping on their own workbench, if you like. And to me Lincolnshire's a nice quiet peaceful county, right out in the country, easy access to motorways to get to and fro, and you have to get away from cricket and relax because it's a non-cricketing county. And as it's turned out the people have been marvellous to me in the village, and it's just a very, very nice part of the world to live.

Williams: And then you've got a flat I think down in Taunton which you share with Viv Richards?

Botham: Well, I did do. Viv and I shared a place together for about six or seven, eight years.

Williams: He's a great mate of yours, isn't he?

Botham: Very, very close, one of my closest friends.

Williams: I'm very interested in this in particular, because you share, I think with me and I hope a lot of people, a sort of blindness to colour. Do you feel strongly about that?

Botham: Yeah, I'm totally against people that think that a man because he's black or yellow or green or whatever is a second-class citizen. As far as I'm concerned I know a lot nicer West Indians than I know Englishmen. And my view is very simple, I treat anybody I meet on how I feel about them. If I don't like a man, well he can be any colour. If I don't like him I have my own reasons for it. And there are very few of those.

Williams: Do you positively go out of your way to try and create a good atmosphere with your West Indian friends?

Botham: No, I just treat them as one of the lads. I treat them the same as I treat David Gower or Bob Willis if they came to my house, doesn't make any difference to me. Viv's also the godfather to my son.

Williams: That's lovely. Just before you go, I'm always fascinated to meet the fringe people in sport. Is it right, for example, that Mick Jagger is a really knowledgeable cricket fan?

Botham: I first met Mick at my first Test match in 1977, and since then we've become pretty good friends. Mick's knowledge of cricket is probably far superior to mine in figures and players and everything.

Williams: You're joking!

Botham: He's totally fanatical on cricket.

Williams: But not on the tactics of the game?

Botham: Well, the strangest conversation I saw in my first Test match was Derek Underwood and Mick Jagger sitting in the corner of the dressing-room discussing field placings for left-arm spinners.

Williams: You said that you won't stay in cricket, you won't just go on and on and on. The impression I get is that you've almost set yourself a time limit and you're going to play as well as you can and get as far as you can and then there'll be a moment when you'll say that's enough.

Botham: I wouldn't say a time limit. It's always been my philosophy in life that there's nothing worse than seeing a sportsman, in any sport, trying to play in his late thirties, forties, when it is obvious to everybody that he's –

Williams: The inspiration's gone.

Botham: Well, he's not the player he was! His reactions have slowed down, everything. And there's certainly no way I'd do that. No, I'd like to get out on a high note, and I think I owe that to myself and more so to the public.

*   *   *

Graeme Pollock

Light Programme, August 1965
Brian Johnston: Graeme, looking back, can you remember when you first started playing cricket, what sort of age?

Graeme Pollock: Well, I've been told by Mother that I started when I was about two or three. I was playing around on the back lawn with a little bat and she was bowling to me.

Johnston: She was a pretty good bowler, was she?

Pollock: Oh yes, she turned them a bit.

Johnston: Has there ever been any sort of rivalry between you and Peter? He's the elder brother, of course. He's the fast bowler and you're the brilliant batsman.

Pollock: Well, when we started playing in junior cricket Peter used to be an opening batsman and I used to be the quickie. But it's changed around a bit now, so I don't think we've really had any rivalry.

Johnston: Did you ever have any serious coaching or were you more or less left alone?

Pollock: The first coach we had was George Cox who played for Sussex. He came out every year and coached at school and I think he helped a lot in letting me play my natural game. He didn't change me too much, I don't think.

Johnston: Have you found the pitches here very different to your South African ones, and perhaps not as good as they might be?

Pollock: Yes, they are different to ours. The main difference is we don't get very much seam in South Africa, whereas over here the ball does definitely move around off the wicket. But I think, if you're prepared to play strokes you can play them on any wicket.

Johnston: Graeme, you don't get a tremendous opportunity for a lot of cricket in South Africa. Is there any chance of your coming over here to play, either in League cricket or for a county?

Pollock: I don't think I would, no. I've got a pretty good job at home and I don't think I could play cricket for twelve months a year. I think a six-month break does me a lot of good and I'm keen to get back to it when our cricket season starts again.

*   *   *

Barry Richards

Sports Magazine, July 1976
Gerald Sinstadt: To some extent cricketing ability can be measured. Batting and bowling averages taken over a period do represent a player's achievement. But there can be subjective approaches too. Cricketers themselves don't need statistics to back up their appraisal of the way a man performs at the highest level. On both counts Barry Richards, the South African batsman now playing for Hampshire, comes very close to the top. Many experts indeed rate him the best batsman in the world today.

Ron Jones has been talking to Richards about his approach to batting. Does he, for example, stand at the crease and try to read the bowler's mind?

Barry Richards: Yes. But that can be dangerous too because you can overread it, if you know what I mean. You can think that he's going to bowl a certain ball and premeditate your shot, and this in nine times out of ten leads to absolute disaster. It does work, particularly in a Sunday game where, towards the end of the 40 overs, chaps are looking to try and cart the ball out of the ground and they premeditate or try and think along the lines of the bowler and get themselves into a position. It does work periodically, but I'd say that 75–80% of the time you will only get yourself into a terrible tangle by trying to premeditate, so I wouldn't advise that at all.

Ron Jones: I've heard you described as one of the most natural batsmen in the world. How much of your reaction to a bowler is natural and how much is practice?

Richards: I don't term myself a natural player, I wouldn't say I was a natural cricketer. I think I'm a grooved cricketer. I've practised a certain technique which, good or bad, came out of a coaching book. I'm more like that than a flair player like Viv Richards. He's not technically correct, but he's got all the flair in the world and lots of natural ability, probably far more than I've got. It's just that my technique's a little bit more sort of grooved and 'coaching manualish'. Whether that's good or bad I don't know. It probably works for me, and will probably work for quite a few people, but not everybody.

Jones: But there must be something of pure Barry Richards in the strokes you deliver and the style of play you have that's not from the book?

Richards: Yes and no. It's difficult to say whether you've got your own particular style. You just see a ball coming towards you and you play how you've practised to play that particular shot. If people associate a particular shot with you, well then you are obviously playing that shot with a certain amount of your own ability. I try and keep my game as all round the wicket as I can possibly get because you can then score in every direction – although I feel I'm naturally more dominant on the off side.

Jones: How would you approach a particular type of bowling? Let's take the fast bowler first.

Richards: It depends where I'm playing him. If I was playing him on a good wicket on a nice day, well then, I'd basically be looking to play him – unless he was super quick, like Andy Roberts – off the front foot. But if we got a hard bouncy wicket then I'd probably play him more off the back foot. A spinner again – if it's an easy wicket and it's the first day of the match and it hasn't taken turn, then I'll essentially be playing off the front foot. If it's turning, particularly a left-arm spinner going away from the right-hand batsman, I might play more off the back foot. It works for me but it might not work for chaps who are not six foot tall. I'm six foot tall, so I can probably stretch more than David Turner, who's only 5′ 6″. You know – different fellows, different techniques.

*   *   *

Richard Hadlee

Sport on Two, September 1984
Richard Hadlee: People tended to treat you as public property. They expected and demanded you to turn up and do speaking engagements and presentations, book promotions, various other publicity stunts, radio and newspaper columns. There were deadlines to meet and I was flying to work and I may have been in Auckland at nine o'clock in the morning and at twelve o'clock I'd be in Wellington, which is another plane flight, and then get home the same day. And everything started to get on top of me and that wasn't even cricket. [*Richard Hadlee explaining the media pressures that are the price of success.*]

I had to start thinking of training and the forthcoming series against England but I just got to the stage where I just lost the desire to do anything. And I didn't have the energy to get up and run round the park, and the end result was that we had to get away from people and telephones and deadlines and pressures, so we went to Rarotonga for a week/ten days, which was absolutely marvellous. Come back a lot better though not quite right because I was having dizzy spells and headaches and blurred vision. It was an unbelievable time. There were even doubts as to whether I'd play cricket again that season.

How I got out of it I don't know, really. I played against England that series, it went quite well. We won a Test match, I got 99 [*2nd Test at Christchurch, February 1984; he also took 8 wickets*] – perhaps I should have got a hundred there – named man of the series, then went on to Sri Lanka and again we won the Test series there and the one-day Internationals. Named man of the series as well, so I started to get everything back again. The adrenalin was flowing and, of course, this county cricket season's been quite outstanding for me. The dreams that I thought about have become reality.

Andy Smith: What you're saying is, the best all-rounder in the world very nearly cracked up?

Hadlee: Well yes, that's right. Because of the pressures and the expectations. I found it very difficult to cope with them. I think the biggest lesson I've learnt from that now is to start saying no when people want me to do this, that and everything else. There are some things that I have to do or need to do but there's other things I'm just going to have to say no to, and, of course, a lot of people may not understand or appreciate that, and it may not help my image actually if I start declining things. Unfortunately one's got to look after health and my health deteriorated badly. Thankfully I'm in tip-top condition now but I just want to avoid another situation like that.

Smith: How much did the family help to pull you out of that, because you are a pretty close-knit family?

Hadlee: Oh, they were very, very worried. My mother came to me one day and she said, 'Richard, you don't look very well. You've just got to have a break. The way you look at present it's as though Mother Nature is telling you to slow down. And if you don't slow down then you may not be with us.' Now that's pretty harsh stuff. That's how worried they were. The way I got out of it was to go on a motivation course – the power of positive thinking that came out of that course gave me a renewed and refreshed outlook on life and things that I had to do, and that's been one of the key factors that's helped me do the double. The will and desire to want to achieve something. Winners make it happen, losers let it happen, type of thing.

To sum up, my profession is cricket and I look for consistency. Which means you've got to bowl a good line and a good length and you've got to be reasonably consistent with the batting. You expect consistency from team-mates, and from umpires as far as decision making is concerned. So all these things, I'm constantly thinking cricket, on and off the field. As soon as one day is over I'm thinking, right, what am I going to do tomorrow? So cricket becomes an obsession if you like, the same as the double thing was. The things I've got to do, got to achieve in this game before I can get out of it.

And when I get out of it I can look back and say, I've been very happy with my career. I've worked hard, I've been rewarded, and in some ways I'll be greatly relieved when it's over. Because then I won't have to train, I won't have to pitch up at the cricket ground, I won't have to tour. There are other things that I'd like to do like camping and fishing and shooting and lie in on a Saturday or Sunday morning in winter. Come home to an open fireplace – I haven't had a winter now for seven or eight years and it's something that I miss.

Smith: But what happened to the Richard Hadlee that used to be in the Tavern at Trent Bridge and would occasionally from the corner of the bar issue a Basil Brush impression? What happened to him? Has Basil gone for ever?

Hadlee: I know what you're getting at – you want one! Tell you what. Hang on. I'll just have another beer and see what I can do for you.

Ha, ha, ha, ha – boom, boom, ha, ha, ha, ha!

*   *   *

AND NOW OVER TO . . .

The fact that good commentary sounds easy usually means that it is not; to be able to make the relevant remark naturally and instantaneously, to formulate and then convey a word picture, is a gift given to few.

In the 1930s, Howard Marshall distinguished many a cricketing occasion, not least with his daily ten-minute summaries at the close of play.

Gentlemen v. Players 1933
Howard Marshall

Wednesday 19 July 1933

We have had an exhilarating day's play in the Gentlemen v. Players match here at Lord's. It has been interesting. We have had glorious weather, and the present position is that the Players, who won the toss, have scored 264 for 9 wickets on an easy-paced pitch.

We started off with a flash, for Barnett, the brilliant Gloucester batsman who went in first with Sutcliffe, cracked the first ball of the match, from Farnes, sparklingly through the covers for four. Farnes was bowling at the pavilion end, by the way, and Barnett chopped the second ball for two, and then to our surprise he played over the top of the third – a yorker, in fact – and he was bowled neck and crop. Well, that was a good man out, and we were hoping to see some lively batting.

Hammond was next, and he seemed to be seeing the ball right away. He drove H. T. O. Smith sharply past mid off to the mound railing. Smith, incidentally, is the Essex fast-medium bowler who came in for R. W. V. Robins. Hammond was in the sort of mood when he apparently regards the bowling as so much practice, and once when a ball was pitched on the leg stump he flicked it contemptuously away over short leg's head to the square-leg boundary. At 25 Jardine, with much reorganising of the field, brought Marriott on for Smith at the Nursery end, and once more the unexpected happened. Hammond played tentatively forward at the last ball of the over – a beautiful-length ball which turned away. He missed it, lifted his right foot, and was finely stumped by Oldfield. Hammond had made 17, and 2 wickets were down for 25 after half an hour, and the Gentlemen, as you may imagine, were very much on their toes.

Marriott, who would be just about the best spin bowler in the country if he played more regularly, was bowling to a couple of slips, a deep and square point, a silly point, cover, mid off, short leg, mid on, and one man deep and fairly straight. In his next over the Players suffered another horrid shock: Sutcliffe played Marriott to Owen-Smith at deepest point, and Leyland scampered up the pitch but was too late and he was run out – Owen-Smith of all men was the wrong man to take such a risk with – and the Players had lost 3 wickets for 28 runs after 35 minutes play.

There was still plenty of good batting to come, and with Watson of Lancashire, who is a good man in situations like this, at one end, and with Sutcliffe digging himself in at the other end – a little uncertainly, it is true – the Gentlemen were by no means through their troubles. Sutcliffe was laborious over his strokes; he seemed to suspect that the wicket was helping Marriott to produce his spin. Both Sutcliffe and Watson kept going up and giving the pitch ruminative pats, and once Watson edged Marriott just short of the slips.

In the meanwhile Fender had come on at the pavilion end, and the 50 went up after exactly an hour. It was very pleasant sitting high up in the Mound Stand in the sunshine, with a little breeze from the south to cool us and the slow rhythm of the game below – and I must admit that I did feel lazy hereabouts. Fender and Marriott were trundling steadily and Sutcliffe and Watson were tapping and patting and taking an occasional run, and somnolence was agreeably in the air. For all that, other spectators were alert enough; they fervently clapped Fender when he wheeled up maiden overs. But it was nearly 1 o'clock before I sat up, to see Sutcliffe play a half-hearted skier off Marriott to Turnbull. That was 67 for 4, and Sutcliffe had made 19.

Really the Gentlemen were doing very well, and Farnes came back at the Pavilion end to greet Langridge, who on one occasion edged him very nearly to Jardine in the gully. Later Langridge gave a chance off Owen-Smith, but it was an awkward catch travelling hard, and then the batsmen seemed to think this was enough until the luncheon interval, which was taken with the score at 87 for 4.

Well, not many people would have imagined that state of affairs. No doubt Sutcliffe had given his orders, but it made the bowling look unutterably difficult. Then after the luncheon interval Farnes, at the Pavilion end, made the ball turn for the first time, and Watson ducked to a rising ball that tapped his glove and he was caught at the wicket by Oldfield after putting together 35 runs in 1½ hours. And that was 5 down for 91, and the Players were in trouble.

Ames came in to stop the rot. I don't know why I particularly noticed it – his brand-new bat – as he walked to the wicket, but I did. He had some fine bowls from Farnes, and an excellent over from Marriott. Farnes, though, did not appear to be really troubling them, and at 104 Jardine put Owen-Smith on, and both Ames and Langridge put the shutters up. By 3 o'clock the crowd became a little restive, and the gentlemen in the grandstand emitted raucous laughter as the ball quietly hit the bat. Marriott was bowling well, but he and Owen-Smith could not seem to get the wicket to help them.

161

At any rate the batsmen picked and brought off firm-footed strokes, making no attempt to knock the bowlers off their length. I suppose they were playing to orders but it was depressing, to put it very mildly, when men fixed themselves and were content to stand and poke.

Well, the 150 went up at a quarter to four – 63 runs scored in 1½ hours after the interval, and then Fender cheered us up by flinging himself full-length to a chance from Ames in the slips. Next Langridge gave a chance to mid off and mid off put it on the floor, and Langridge celebrated his little luck by finely playing a ball off Marriott to the boundary over mid on's head. Then Ames livened the play up a bit and reached his 50 at 4 o'clock – he generally seems to make runs on the big occasions at Lord's. Langridge also reached his 50 before the tea interval – he had taken 2 hours 45 minutes over this, and not three weeks as someone in the crowd remarked – and to give Ames and Langridge their due they had pulled the Players out of a very nasty hole. Tea – 221 for 5 – quite a different story from 91 for 5 at twenty minutes past two.

After tea, whilst the other bowlers only served to keep the batsmen quieter it was H. T. O. Smith who broke up the partnership by getting Ames at 238. Ames had made 82, and he and Langridge had put on 147 in 2 hours and 40 minutes. An invaluable stand for the Players. Then Wyatt, who had changed over to the Nursery end, did his bit by getting the patient Langridge lbw with the total at 240. Langridge had been in 3½ hours, and the Players had lost 7 wickets.

After that the end was pretty well in sight. Jardine at silly point picked a ball from Marriott almost off Townsend's bat; Verity was soon out lbw to Marriott; and now it is just on half past six and the score is – Players 278 – Nichols 10, Clark 13.

Thursday 20 July 1933

This has been rather a sad day for the Gentlemen in their match against the Players here at Lord's. The Players carried their total to 309, and then rattled the Gentlemen out for 143. The Gentlemen have followed on, and now they have made 145 for the loss of 6 wickets.

It was an odd steamy sort of morning when Nichols and Clark came out to continue the Players' innings. There was a strong sun lurking behind the clouds and I am told that earlier in the day – about 7 – the tail-end of a thunderstorm had drenched the pitch for twenty minutes or so. We expected the pitch to be a bit difficult, but Nichols and Clark added 47 runs for the last wicket before Nichols was run out.

The Players' total of 309 was very respectable considering how badly their innings had started. It was a quarter to one when Walters and Wyatt came out from the Pavilion to face the attack of Clark, the Northants fast left-hander, from the Nursery end. Clark made the ball lift right away, which suggested that there would be some life in the game, and Wyatt took a nasty rap on the knuckles, and in the next over a bumpy one got his ribs, and with 17 runs on the board he tried to hook a short ball from Nichols, played his stroke too late, and was easily caught off the splice by Barnett at mid on.

This was a discouraging start for the Gentlemen, whose batting is by no means solid all the way down, and 12 runs later Nichols made one rise sharply and the Nawab of Pataudi, playing forward without getting to the pitch of the ball, was caught off his gloves by Ames behind the wicket. With 29 runs and 2 wickets down things didn't look too good.

Just about then the sun came out strongly and Sutcliffe made a double bowling change, bringing Verity on at the Nursery end and Townsend at the other, bowling round the wicket with three short legs. Verity soon troubled Walters, and with the total at 33 caught him in two minds with a ball of perfect length which turned away sharply, and Walters edged it into Watson's hands at slip. He had been in an hour for his 11 runs.

Now it was up to Jardine to stop the rot. Jardine was certainly the man for the occasion, but Turnbull in the meantime was not afraid to use his bat. It was refreshing to see him go down the pitch to Nichols and Townsend. Soon after this Townsend brought up another short leg – he had four of them in a circle about five yards from Jardine's bat – and once Jardine very nearly put up a catch which brought an excited gasp from the crowd. Then Turnbull's initiative betrayed him. Turnbull lashed out to Verity and drove the ball firm into Sutcliffe's hands at cover. Four wickets down and only 38 runs on the board, and the game seemed to be petering out.

It looked even more grim when Owen-Smith, aggressive as ever, had ballooned a catch off Townsend to Barnett in the deep. Fender had been given lbw to Townsend, and Hammond at slip to Verity had picked the ball pretty well off Oldfield's bat, so that 7 wickets had fallen for 53. And the Players naturally came jubilantly into lunch. A good morning's work. But it had been a disappointing morning in a way, making every allowance for some steady bowling by Townsend and Verity on a lively wicket.

When H. T. O. Smith was run out soon after the interval we thought the end had come, but we had reckoned without our Jardine. He began to bat superbly, driving both Townsend and Verity to the long-on boundary and forcing Townsend to have three men out as well as his ring of policemen. Jardine chopped Townsend towards a non-existent third man for a couple and drove Verity for four – 'This was more like it,' we said to one another – and then Sutcliffe decided that more pace was needed and he brought Clark on at the Pavilion end.

Hereabouts Farnes sent up the 100 with a fine drive off Verity over mid on's head. Things were becoming really interesting: the Players were on their toes; Jardine and Farnes were not the least perturbed; there was venom in the bowling and spirit in the batting and the crowd appreciated it all thoroughly. There were cheers as Jardine cunningly stole the bowling time after time, and meanwhile Farnes was playing as good an innings, hitting the ball with the middle of the bat and resisting all temptations. Runs kept coming steadily – Jardine reached his 50 amid loud applause – 19 more were needed to save the follow-on – and then suddenly Jardine played forward to a ball from Langridge, missed it, and was brilliantly stumped by Ames. An unexpected end to a superb innings – one of the best that Jardine has played. He had made 59 runs, and his partnership with Farnes had put on 78 invaluable runs. But unfortunately for the Gentlemen they had shot their bolt. Marriott was soon out to Nichols, so that the innings closed for 143, which was 166 behind the Players.

Naturally the Gentlemen had to follow on. They began their second innings at 3.40 and with only 5 on the board Nichols from the Nursery end brought one back to bowl Walters lock, stock and barrel. Another poor start, and when Nichols did the same to Pataudi 10 runs later, sending his off stump madly through the air, it didn't seem there was much hope. Still, Wyatt was playing very well – he hooked short ones from Nichols and Clark with admirable judgement and seemed confident against all the bowling.

Sutcliffe tried Hammond at the Nursery end Langridge at the other but it made no difference, and soon the old firm, Verity and Townsend, returned to the attack. Then Wyatt played a somewhat less confident stroke straight back to Townsend and was caught and bowled. Three down for 45, and Jardine stepped into the breach once more.

After that the cricket became rather somnolent. Now and again the batsman would force the ball away – Turnbull especially making some pleasing strokes – but they were taking no risks, and the score slowly crept to 90 before Jardine was out lbw to Langridge after making 19 runs. The whole game, as a matter of fact, had become rather patient, as if the Gentlemen were not very hopeful, and the Players tired after their long day in the field. Turnbull, though, sent the 100 up with a lusty pull to the square-leg boundary off Langridge. He kept on batting admirably until he was 72, and then Verity had him lbw with the total 129. It was a fine innings of Turnbull's, but the Gentlemen were a long way from being out of the wood, and before long Fender failed to get hold of one from Verity and gave a simple catch to Sutcliffe at mid off. That was 6 for 145.

And now from my window here at Lord's I see they have just stopped the game, pulled up stumps, and the final score is Gentlemen, 2nd innings, 152 for 6, Owen-Smith not out 24, Oldfield not out 0. I will just repeat that the Gentlemen in their first innings were all out for 143.

Friday 21 July 1933
Well, you will remember, I expect, that this morning the Gentlemen, with 4 wickets to fall, still needed 14 runs to save them from the innings defeat against the Players. Well, they got their 14 runs – and a few more – but they were all out for 177, and by mid-day the Players had won a somewhat disappointing match by the large margin of 10 wickets.

Naturally we did not expect great things when we went along to Lord's this morning, but Owen-Smith was still in and, if he could find someone to stay with while he batted with his proper pugnacity, there was an outside chance that the Gentlemen might save the game. It was very much of an outside chance, of course, and as it happened Owen-Smith was not in one of his inspired moods when he takes control and makes even the best bowling look harmless.

Sutcliffe began his attack with Verity at the Nursery end and Nichols at the other, and when Verity had had a couple of overs and found there was no bite in the pitch, Clark came on instead to bowl his fastish left-hand stuff. For some time the batsmen were quiet; they evaded trouble, and Oldfield's guardian angel steered his bat out of the way of several rising balls outside the off stump. Owen-Smith was in no sort of a hurry, but he did surprise Nichols by flicking his bat very late at a good-length ball and driving it over Nichols' head bang up against the Pavilion railings, whereupon Nichols registered his displeasure by bowling a wide.

Still, that was only a pleasant interlude. For twenty-five minutes nothing much happened, and then Clark was justly rewarded. He had industriously made the ball run away from the bat, and suddenly Owen-Smith edged one and the infallible Hammond held the catch at second slip. Then the little gathering of faithful spectators sighed and gathered up their belongings and put on their hats – for the match was as good as over. Clark bowled H. T. O. Smith with a ball pitched on the leg stump which took the top of the middle stump, and after he had also disposed of Oldfield in the same way, Nichols bowled Farnes, and the Gentlemen were all out for 177.

That left the Players 12 runs to make. Verity and Barnett set about the job confidently enough. Verity is a useful opening batsman, and he played Marriott with professional dignity while Barnett collected the runs. And Barnett did the thing in style – he banged Fender gloriously through the covers and then in the same over he jumped down the pitch and punched the ball like lightning past extra cover to the boundary. That was the winning hit, and a very worthy one. Barnett had the minor distinction of scoring four runs off the first and the last balls of the match – that is some indication of his methods and temperament.

Well, there it is. Not, I am afraid, an altogether satisfactory story from the amateur point of view. It is quite true that the Gentlemen started well, and if only a couple of catches had been held, the Langridge–Ames partnership would have been cut short and the Players' total might have looked very different. And then that thunderstorm early yesterday morning, which made the wicket just right for Verity and Townsend – that was hard on the Gentlemen, I must admit. But for all that there is no getting away from it this was a pretty indifferent Gentlemen's side, with C. S. Marriott the only bowler of class, and the batting, after Jardine, extremely doubtful.

I did not have time yesterday evening to say as much as I could have wished about Jardine's innings of 59, but it was a superb performance and quite the best thing of the match. There is no doubt that when Jardine came in, with the Gentlemen's wickets tumbling like ninepins, the pitch was very eccentric. There was a good deal of moisture in it and the sun had just got fiercely to work, and Verity particularly was spinning the ball viciously – he spun it so much, as a matter of fact, that it found the edge of even Jardine's meticulously straight bat more than once – but Jardine stayed there grimly until the luncheon interval. Afterwards the wicket became gradually faster and easier, and Jardine grew correspondingly more aggressive and brilliant. The point which interested me most about Jardine's innings was the range of strokes he produced – off drives, square cuts, powerful pulls and hooks. He showed himself, in fact, to be what we know him to be, although he does not often show us the complete batsman; he so often does limit himself to on-side play with occasional late cuts as a variation. I wish we could see more of this masterful generous Jardine, if only as an example to the cramped restricted modern player.

It was good to find Turnbull meeting spin bowlers with swift footwork, though his methods showed up the tortured firm-footed hesitancy of most of the other amateurs, who allowed Verity and Townsend to dictate a length to them. Still, how workmanlike these professional bowlers are. This was another point which the game brought out – the admirably competent way they set about their attack, taking every advantage of the changing turf, sending down no ball without purpose behind it. There is something closely knit and concentrated about the professional attack which the amateurs miss. But mind you, Marriott on Wednesday was extremely good; his control of length and spin were most impressive.

By the same token some of the Players' batting was disappointing. Sutcliffe has not run into form yet, although I hope he will in the Test match which begins tomorrow [*2nd Test v. West Indies at Old Trafford. Sutcliffe was run out for 20 but Jardine made a century in a drawn match*]. Barnett, Hammond and Leyland were out before we had time to look at them properly. Ames and Langridge saved the Players from a horrible collapse, but they went on consciously saving them by dull and unenterprising cricket long after the tide had turned. On the whole, then, it has not been a great match, although it has had its great moments – and at least the weather was glorious. May that be a propitious omen for the next four days at Old Trafford.

*   *   *   *

During the rain-affected Fifth Test match at the Oval in 1977 between England and Australia, the incomparable John Arlott demonstrated in masterly fashion how to deal with those moments all commentators dread. Play is imminent and yet there is nothing happening on the field – well, very nearly nothing –

England v. Australia, Fifth Test 1977

Radio 3, 27 August 1977
John Arlott: And there goes one cover. The second one following it. They're being towed away now down to the Vauxhall End. One of the men has dropped out and come back with the groundsman himself to get the third one off, but we still shan't get an 11.30 start, and of course we can expect that at almost any moment there will be a stoppage between the two innings. About 11.32 now, 33 perhaps. One more cover to come off, and there's no reason that I can see why the players themselves couldn't come out while there's still that one cover to be removed. The pitch obviously is dry. It's not been a really wet night in London by any means. Rain in some quarters, but not everywhere, although I hear that down in Sussex this morning there was extremely heavy rain. Well, two of the covers are away over the boundary rope down at the Vauxhall End, in their various places, and now three – the first three in – coming out to fetch the last of the covers. Still no sign from the players or the umpires. The umpires presumably have come back in to put their coats on. They've got two flights of stairs to climb, and it looks as if – with all being done in leisurely fashion – the start may be ten minutes late. There's two ground-staff men coming out now to take that cover off, and presumably someone must put the stumps into position. It looks as if the groundsman himself is going to come out and do that. The creases have been sharply and clearly marked, and I don't know – I didn't see. Bill, did you? – was the pitch by any chance rolled this morning before the covers were put back on?

Bill Frindall: I didn't notice it being rolled, John, but I wasn't watching all the time.

Arlott: No sign of a roller coming out. That spell of rain, I would think, didn't last half a minute, and it's now held up proceedings by over five minutes. I think it must have been rolled early on. Either that or Brearley didn't want a roller because there's just this one England wicket to fall. It's 181 for nine – with Willis 6 and Hendrick 1. There goes the last cover. The groundsman putting in the stumps. Quite a large crowd. There's barely a vacant seat to be seen, except some of those reserved seats where no doubt tickets have been sold and the ticket-holders haven't yet arrived. But otherwise on the popular side there's barely a gap to be seen. The ground won't hold as many in these days as it used to of old because sitting out on the grass is no longer permitted, alas! It used to make for a better gate and a very happy atmosphere, until there was so much hooliganism from people who'd come out on the pitch, that they had to be barred from the ground altogether. The stumps are in position then, the groundsman walking away, and we await the appearance of the umpires, and as I say, this is of extreme importance, because if there were another scud of rain now they could cover all over again. So. To what do you attribute the delay, Fred?

Fred Trueman: Good morning, everyone. Just the delay, just getting the covers off, that's all. The umpires ought to be there now, I mean.

Arlott: Well, that's what I say. I mean, the covers have been off for several minutes.

Trueman: Oh yes, you were quite right, what you were saying earlier, that you thought the umpires and the players would have come out while the last cover was being removed, and got cracking. This is one of the little things that do infuriate people – spectators – these silly little delays like this where, with a little bit of initiative, the players could have been out there as the last cover was being removed. Which should have been fairly easy. I was surprised the covers went on, actually, because it was very light spotting rain. I don't think there was any need for all that covering when it was nothing, was it?

Arlott: No.

Trueman: It was practically in the wind, whatever it was.

Arlott: Well, I would have thought there were about six or eight spots on this large window-pane and that was all. It probably went on for half a minute.

There again an appeal for people not to come on the playing area. You can probably hear the secretary appealing now for people not to move, particularly in the tall stand at the Vauxhall end, and it was there that there was an awful lot of trouble yesterday. On one occasion a gang of about six men seemed to wait for Malone to be ready to start an over, and then they walked the length of the stand, which is fairly considerable, holding up proceedings while they did so. Anyway, the umpires have the bails on.

Trueman: The players aren't rushing out, are they, John?

Arlott: Do you think the ball will swing about today, as it did yesterday, Fred?

Trueman: I don't know. There's plenty of cloud around. It's – in fact I think it is heavier cloud than yesterday, so it possibly will. I don't know. It was a funny day yesterday, because the ball didn't swing very much before lunch at all, and then about twenty minutes after lunch it suddenly started going all over the place and continued swinging right through to 6.30 last night. Even the second new ball, when they took that one, that swung straightaway. But it is a heavier cloud today. There wasn't much movement off the wicket at all yesterday. It was the swing of the ball in the air that got people out, and we've noticed on this trip, if you remember the one-day match at Edgbaston, where the ball swung. Cosier and Greg Chappell swung the ball all over the place and England were in trouble, and then England swung the ball and Australia were in trouble.

Arlott: And there's the applause, first for the Australians, then for the two English batsmen coming out; Willis, of course, a former Surrey player. They are very large and strong men indeed, Willis and Hendrick. And Malone trotting away down to the Vauxhall end, and taking the ball off umpire Tom Spencer. He already has the extremely good figures of 5 for 53 in 43 overs [*in his only Test*]. Some immaculate bowling, of perfect length, some swing, no great pace.

And it's Willis to take strike from Malone. Malone bowling from the Vauxhall end, and Chappell making a request of umpire Constant, asking him something about the crease markings. Now Constant comes in, and Chappell appears satisfied. He himself comes down to first slip, with McCosker second, Hughes third, Bright in the gully, Walters at cover, Hookes mid off, Walker mid on, Thomson long leg, Marsh keeping wicket, of course, Serjeant at square leg, just straight of the umpire. And now Chappell's making another change, and he's moving Walker from mid on to mid off, Hookes from mid off to cover, and Walters round to short third man. And up then comes Malone, moves in, bowls to Willis, and Willis plays this one on the on side, and that first single is rapturously greeted, as you heard, and it takes England up to 182. Seven to Willis, one to Hendrick. But what it does mean now is that the pitch can't be covered until play is abandoned for the day, and this might be a considerable tactical advantage to England, if Underwood has the opportunity of bowling on a wet or drying wicket.

England eventually reached 214. Australia replied with 385 but, with the first day washed out, the weather deemed that the match be drawn. England won the series 3–0 and so regained the Ashes.

*   *   *

AN UMPIRE'S LOT

The men in the white coats are usually only noticed when a decision is demanded. However, it is too facile to assume that, as in the case of football referees, the more inconspicuous they are the better they are umpiring. Certainly nobody could help but notice two of the finest umpires of this century – Frank Chester and 'Dicky' Bird.

Harold 'Dicky' Bird

Outlook, World Service, June 1978

John Tidmarsh: Now, if you'll just give me a moment to take a fresh guard and also have the sightscreen moved, I can then introduce our next guest. He's the Test match umpire, 'Dicky' Bird. He'll be a familiar figure to many of you around the world, even if you've only seen him on television. He usually wears a plain white flat cap, and there are times when he seems to be more involved in the cricket than some of the players. In his own cricketing career he played with some success as a batsman, first for Yorkshire and then for Leicestershire, and I asked him if having played the game at that level was an essential qualification for being an umpire.

'Dicky' Bird: It has certainly helped me as a first-class county and Test umpire, there's no question about that. I think that it helps you to sort the problems out when you've played the game. The things that players may try, you've gone through it yourself as a player.

Tidmarsh: What about taking regular medical examinations just to show that you can see and hear?

Bird: It's a funny thing this. We have to have a thorough medical examination every year. Now a football league referee does not have to have a medical. We have. You've got to be really physically fit to stand six and a half hours each day seven days a week.

Tidmarsh: What about the equipment that you take out with you? When I do an odd bit of umpiring in our village cricket, I've got six stones in my pocket to count the balls. What else do you need apart from that?

Bird: Oh, I take everything. I've got my six little miniature red barrels which I carry in my pocket for counting. I have a spare ball, spare bail, a rag to dry the ball on, scissors, pen-knife, safety pins, elastoplast, chewing-gum – you name it, I carry it.

I've a funny story, you know. In a Test match v. India at Old Trafford

[*1974*], Sunil Gavaskar, the Indian opening batsman, asked me, 'Dicky, have you any scissors?' And I said, 'Why, Sunny?' He said, 'I'd like you to clip the hair, because it's dropping in my eyes.' And I gave him a real short back and sides, and he said, 'I won't need a haircut now for six months at least, Dicky.'

Tidmarsh: I can't let you go without telling your favourite story.

Bird: I think my name, Dicky Bird, attracted the West Indies supporters. I, as you know, wear a white cap and the West Indies supporters have pinched more white caps of mine – honestly, they seem to just whip them off my head, like shelling peas.

And I caught a bus from Hyde Park to Lord's and this big West Indian conductor was coming round. 'Fares please, fares please.' And I looked at him and he had this white cap on. And I said to him, 'Excuse me, sir, where did you get that white cap?' And he said, 'White cap? Man, have you heard of Massa Dicky Bird, the umpire? Dis is one of his white caps, man.' And I didn't let on who I was and I thought how funny, there he was, a bus conductor in the middle of London, and he had one of my white caps on. I thought that was very, very amusing.

*　　　*　　　*

Retirement of Frank Chester

November 1955
Eamonn Andrews: I believe you feel that umpiring cricket matches is one of the most strenuous tasks?

Frank Chester: Yes, I personally think that umpiring cricket matches is one of the hardest jobs in sport. Sometimes I've stood for seven hours a day, and the concentration factor is very, very strenuous indeed.

Andrews: You were a football referee as well?

Chester: Yes. I've done two years of refereeing. That's why I compare the two.

Andrews: When did you take up umpiring?

Chester: I was appointed onto the first-class umpires list in 1921. Before that I'd had two years qualification for Worcestershire, and when I was qualified I played for them and got my cap in 1912.

Andrews: How old were you then?

Chester: I was only sixteen years and a half. And then I played in 1913 and 1914 and then, as everybody knows, the First World War started. I joined the Army and in 1917 I lost my right arm.

Andrews: And then you wanted to stay in cricket and the only way to stay in was as an umpire?

Chester: Exactly, yes. I've had thirty-four years as an umpire on the first-class list.

Andrews: Can you pick out some of the outstanding players that you've come across in that time?

Chester: There's so many great players that I've seen. I umpired a match a few years ago at Lord's – India playing England [1952] – and there was a great performance by Vinoo Mankad. I don't think I've seen anything better. He got a hundred and he got 80 and he bowled practically throughout the England innings. That was a great performance.

Andrews: Apart from Mankad, who would you say was the outstanding batsman?

Chester: Well, personally I think Jack Hobbs is the greatest batsman I've ever seen. The next one, of course, is Sir Donald Bradman. Sir Donald Bradman was a very, very hard man to keep quiet. He was a run-getting machine. They're the greatest batsmen I've ever seen.

March 1956
Sir Donald Bradman: I can remember quite vividly two exceptional decisions Frank Chester gave. In the First Test at Nottingham in 1938 I played at a ball from Sinfield. It span back from the off, very faintly touched the inside edge of my bat, hit the top of my pad, went over the middle stump and, as I slightly overbalanced, Les Ames whipped the bails off and appealed to the square-leg umpire for stumping. I hastily looked around to see the umpire shake his head. This, coupled with the knowledge that I hadn't been bowled made me momentarily breathe a sigh of relief. Ames appealed to Chester at the bowler's end, obviously for caught or lbw. At once Chester nonchalantly said, 'Out, caught!' It was a superb decision, one which tested all the qualities of an umpire.

Then I recall a match at Folkestone, where our wicket-keeper took the ball following a faint click and both he and the nearby fieldsman appealed, thinking the batsman had hit the ball. Chester calmly raised his finger and said, 'Out, lbw!' I thought he had made a mistake until I questioned the batsman, who affirmed that the ball had just touched his pad not his bat and he was quite satisfied he was out lbw.

Those were just two of many outstanding decisions which I saw Chester give. The unhurried, masterful way he pronounced judgement on the most difficult appeals stamped him, in my opinion, as the finest umpire of his period.

April 1956

'Gubby' Allen: As long ago as 1925, I can remember seeing Frank Chester give a brilliant decision. It was when I was playing for Middlesex against Yorkshire in Roy Kilner's benefit match – Roy Kilner, that charming and great Yorkshireman whose early death was a tragedy. Well, in this match, in one of my early overs, Herbert Sutcliffe played at one. There was a loud click and I distinctly saw the ball change course. All our players appealed and to our horror Frank said, 'Not out!' At the end of the over he said, 'Now, Mr Allen, I know you're disappointed. Come down to the other end with me quickly.' He walked straight up to the stumps and pointed at the off stump, and there, sure enough, on the off stump, there was a little red mark made by the ball. He said, 'There you are. I was right.'

Now that was an amazing decision, because the ball clearly changed its course, and yet he had the eyesight to see that it had missed the bat and he had the confidence to abide by his opinion. It was a very great decision that could only have been given by perhaps the greatest umpire of all time. Herbert Sutcliffe, I might say, had made 7 at the time and he went on to make 200. So you can imagine we didn't really feel quite so kindly towards Frank that day as we might have done.

*   *   *

QUESTION AND ANSWER

The 'unashamedly bland' approach of the 'Gentle Giant', as John Dunn is affectionately known in radio circles, often succeeds in soliciting from the interviewee far more than he or she had intended to reveal. A couple of decades after his tribute to Frank Chester, Gubby Allen, who has embraced cricket in so many spheres, returned to the studio to be forthcoming on his own career.

'Gubby' Allen

John Dunn Show, April 1985

Gubby Allen: I maintain that everybody who gets anywhere in life has a bit of luck. Much to my fury I was sent to Eton by my father, and just at the most important moment in my cricketing career the famous George Hirst – a lovely man – turned up as the coach. Now he was the first-ever fast bowler who swung the ball.

Now, as a little kid I could always swing the ball – I didn't know why, but I could – and George turned up and, of course, he taught me all about it. It was luck and luck goes everywhere through my life.

I wasn't picked for the first Test match I played in, but Larwood breaks down, so I'm pulled in. Didn't have a very good match, made some runs but got left out, and it looked perhaps as though my cricket career was gone. Not at all. The next year Larwood was ill again and I got pulled in again. This time I didn't bowl very well but I happened to make a hundred. So then they couldn't leave me out. So luck is a terrific thing.

John Dunn: Most people when they are at school have cricketing heroes. Who were your heroes?

Allen: Oh, I think Jack Hobbs. Mind you, I think my first hero was the first cricketer I ever met. I was taken to my first Test match when I was just about ten. We went to the Oval to see England play South Africa, simply because Reggie Spooner, who was the only famous cricketer I knew at that time, was playing and he holed out at deep square leg off a full pitch, and I burst into tears – or so the family said. This has always been a family joke against me. When we got home Father said, 'You know, I don't think you ought to burst into tears just because a friend of yours gets out.' I said, 'It wasn't because he got out. It was because he played such a terrible stroke!'

Dunn: It's a good yarn! You were an amateur, were you not?

Allen: Yes. I had to work for my living and I played whenever I could get away.

Dunn: What was your job?

Allen: Oh, I had three jobs. I first started in insurance, then I went into Debenhams for a few years, and then when I came back from Australia I became a stockbroker and was a stockbroker for the rest of my life. But I had to work. It did limit my fitness.

Dunn: You went on tours, even to Argentina. I didn't know we played cricket against Argentina. Mostly expats, I suppose?

Allen: Yes. In those days they were quite good. I remember going on to Valparaiso and there was an earth tremor and it knocked the bails off and everybody had to lay on the ground. I got up and had to bowl the next ball. The chap hooked me for six!

Dunn: Now, let's come on to this infamous tour, the 'Bodyline' series. You have always been known as the fast bowler who would not bowl bodyline. But I think Jardine asked you to, didn't he?

Allen: Oh yes. Well, that story's been told so many times. It's quite true that he did and I just said that I wouldn't do it. If we went into that we'd be here all night, but I didn't think it was the right way to play cricket.

It was in the second innings of the Second Test match that, in my opinion, bodyline really developed. I don't think it was planned – I've always said that. I think it was talked about. There was no doubt – there was the famous dinner at the Piccadilly Hotel, or wherever it was, and Douglas [*Jardine*] talked to Harold [*Larwood*] and Bill Voce about it and they were really talking more about leg theory. But as the tour went on it developed. I'm absolutely convinced that's right.

Dunn: But didn't Jardine have this hatred for Australians?

Allen: No, he didn't hate Australians, I don't accept that. Douglas was very sensitive but determined to win. On the tour there before, he used to wear that highly-coloured Harlequin cap and they used to get at him a bit. And he never really quite got over that.

Dunn: But was the reason that you were able to say to him, no, I will not obey your commands and bowl bodyline, because you were an amateur? Were Larwood and Voce in the same position?

Allen: Well, that's been said millions of times. But I mean, I wanted to play for England. I should have been very hurt if I'd never been asked to play for England again because I'd done this. I just didn't think it was right, that was all. I'd never bowled it and I wouldn't have been any good at it, anyhow. I thought it was the wrong way to play cricket.

Dunn: How was it abolished?

Allen: Eighteen months later the counties met at Lord's and they told Nottingham that, unless they would give a guarantee not to employ those tactics, nobody was going to play them. It was an absolutely unanimous vote. That was what killed bodyline. If the counties were going to say that, it must have been wrong.

Dunn: Weren't you also of the opinion that it came about because of the lbw laws, in that the batsmen could pad up outside the off stump and they could get away with murder that side and therefore the bowlers were left with nothing but to bowl down the 'body line'?

Allen: Well, I don't know –

Dunn: Because you were also instrumental in changing the lbw law, were you not?

Allen: Yes. I must say that was the worst thing I ever did for cricket. I think that change in the lbw – looking back on it now – was the biggest mistake that's ever been made in cricket administration.

Dunn: Why is that?

Allen: It helps all bowlers, of course. But it encourages, in particular, the man who makes the ball come on to the bat. Consequently the leg-spinner's gone, the old orthodox left-armer is gone, and I think the best thing we could ever do for cricket is to go back to the old lbw law, and widen the wicket a little bit to compensate.

Dunn: After your playing days you were a selector and an administrator and all the rest of it. Have you had as much satisfaction from working off the pitch as when you were playing?

Allen: Oh yes, it's fascinating. I worked very hard at it. I think the thing I'm most proud of is that I did get MCC to set up a Youth Cricket enquiry, which led on to the writing of the coaching manual and all the coaching schemes which now exist.

*   *   *

David Gower

John Dunn Show, October 1983
John Dunn: Let's take boisterous Botham first, because I think he is a close personal friend?

David Gower: Well yes, I've played international cricket with him for about the last five years or so, and you cannot go on tour with Ian Botham without becoming some sort of friend or enemy! He's a lovely man, he's full of energy, dangerous energy at times, but he has been good company.

Dunn: And very competitive.

Gower: Oh yes, he competes at everything. If he is playing tennis or golf or driving through town he's competing. Everything he does is a competition.

Dunn. Yes. But for those days when you're rained off and you're hanging about the dressing-room with nothing very much to do, is he a liability then?

Gower: Can be, yes. There's only one way you can keep him quiet sometimes, and that's just get him playing cards all day. And it needs one volunteer or one good crib player to tie him down for the rest of the day. And that's not a bad system. But if you let him loose, well I've had my newspaper go up in smoke! If you mention anything about it, he'll do it again.

Dunn: And you shared a room with him, of course, in Sydney too?

Gower: I did. Long time ago. And I was very lucky in some ways, because I caught him at a quiet period. He even wrote a letter home to his wife that time!

Dunn. That's unusual, is it?

Gower: Kath isn't used to receiving letters like that, you know!

Dunn: Actually, one doesn't think about that, that when you are on tour you have to share rooms with people. Who decides who shares with whom?

Gower: Well, Bernard Thomas, the England physio, is the man that allocates the rooms. And we operate a system whereby you keep changing round. You stay with a fellow for two weeks, then he sort of changes them round and lets you know who's next, who's the next victim.

Dunn: If two people really don't get on, I presume that they would try and avoid putting them together?

Gower: Well you can, if it gets to that stage, which is very rare. Then it's up to them to say to Bernard, look, I'm sorry, but honestly there is no way I can stay in the same room again for another night.

Dunn: Ian Botham you would call a close personal friend. How would you describe your relationship with Geoffrey Boycott?

Gower: Well, I think anyone's relation with Geoffrey Boycott is going to be up and down. At his best he can be a very, very nice man indeed, and I've learned quite a few things from Geoffrey over the last few years and he was a help to me in early Test days. He's a man with immense cricket knowledge, and if he's prepared to talk about it, then you're going to learn a lot whatever happens. In fact, between us, Ian and Geoff, when Geoff came back from his self-imposed exile from Test cricket, it was Ian really who brought him out of his shell a bit, who ribbed him in the dressing-room. He called him fat. Geoffrey then called Ian Guy the Gorilla. And the two had this mutual respect, knowing that they both play cricket well. It just needed someone to help Geoff become part of the team again. It would have been very easy for him to remain slightly apart.

Dunn: You've shared a wicket, of course, on a number of occasions with him. What is he like when you're batting with him?

Gower: Geoff? He's a rock, isn't he, at the other end. He's a very very solid performer. He's a hard-thinking cricketer, and he's good with advice, he's good with just reminding us how to keep going, what not to do. He can spot things in people, he can see people starting to get loose, when they look as though they might get out and start to change the innings.

Dunn: But is he the boss when you're out there?

Gower: Well, he probably was at that stage, inasmuch as there was a man who was twenty years older than me, or not quite that much perhaps, there was a man substantially older than me, a lot of Test experience, a lot of high-class cricket experience, and I was a young man making my way, new to Test cricket.

Dunn: You think he gave you quite a lot of advice. Is he the sort of person that would give advice to anybody, regardless of whether it was wanted or not? Like a captain, for instance?

Gower: No, he won't impose it on you. He likes, I think, to be asked, he likes to feel needed, and if you catch him right and you ask the right question, then he will go on and do you a favour then.

Dunn: Let's move on to Bob Willis, shall we? Now I would think he's a fairly difficult man to get to know.

Gower: Yes, he is hard to get to know. He doesn't sort of open up straight-away. He's not as obviously friendly as, say, Both. But over the years I have come to know him gradually and come to like him a lot.

Dunn: There's obviously almost a sort of demonic side to him. When you see him running up to bowl sometimes, there's real hate seems to come out of his eyes.

Gower: Oh, there's plenty of fire there. Yes, they are blazing all right. That's been his great contribution for England, that whenever he's got the lions on his sweater and he sets off down the hill somewhere, he is trying his hardest, he is giving his all.

Dunn: Is he an inspiring captain to play under?

Gower: Yes. He leads by example, you know. Obviously he's there at the outset. He's opening the bowling, he's our main strike bowler, and has been for some while.

Dunn: But does he give good pep talks in the dressing-room where necessary?

Gower: He's done it before, yes. It's a hard thing, pep talks, because you can always overdo them. Especially when you are playing cricket every day of the week, where you've got a five-day Test match. If you get a pep talk at the start of every session or the start of every day, whatever you said might start to pale a bit. I think there are times when you need to be jolted, when perhaps even top creamers become slightly casual.

Dunn: Obviously there must be times an individual player might need to be bawled out. Is he good at that as well?

Gower: Oh yes. I remember Bob for instance when he was vice-captain, giving that sort of support. We had a game in Sri Lanka, in fact the inaugural Test match, when we looked in danger of losing. And we came back after the rest day on the fourth morning and it was Bob, in fact, who raised us out of the torpor and set us on the way.

Dunn: Are you sorry that your chance of captaincy is not going to come this winter?

Gower: Now, I wouldn't say that. I mean, I am quite happy to bide my time and do it when I am required.

Dunn: Do you think you can do it? Is it a job that you reckon is inside your compass?

Gower: I think it's possible, yes. It would be very negative thinking to say otherwise.

Dunn: Yes, but you know, there's been so much trouble in recent years, particularly when Ian Botham was made the captain, and one felt that that possibly was one of the reasons we have lost before.

Gower: Well possibly, but also remember that Ian played something like

179

nine out of ten Test matches during his captaincy against the West Indies. And it's not easy against them under most circumstances, and it's very easy to lose form against a side like that.

Dunn: But equally true, the possibility is there that the new captain could be coming in to face the West Indies next summer?

Gower: Well that's . . . yes . . . I mean, perhaps best not to think about that, again that might be negative thinking to look at it that way.

Dunn: I think you're very lucky to be a left-hander.

Gower: Yes, I don't mind being a left-hander. I think there are positive things and bad things.

Dunn: But so many left-handers are more attractive to watch than right-handers. I want to ask you why? Are you left-handed in everything?

Gower: No, I am very much right-handed. If I write you a letter, which is possibly unusual, that would be right-handed, or I play things like tennis, squash and golf right-handed.

Dunn: So were you coached into playing cricket left-handed?

Gower: No, I was left. When I first picked up a bat, at the tender age of three or something, I picked it up left-handed. And my father was tempted I think, so my mother tells me, to make me bat right-handed in the traditional manner and she put her foot down and said no, no, leave him as he is. And I stuck with it that way. So I owe her a lot for that.

Dunn: You had a very good career at school, as well I know. Was that where you decided that you might make a career out of cricket?

Gower: I don't know when I decided that because when I left school, I joined Leicestershire straightaway. I left school at the end of March and joined the club for my first full season. I think it was after that that I really decided that I was going to do it. Because I then went to university for six months, and did very little practical stuff, and returned to Leicestershire straightaway, parted company by mutual consent, and that was the end of university.

Dunn: Why did you go to Leicestershire and not to Kent? Because you were born in Tunbridge Wells?

Gower: Yes. I never actually lived in Kent really, apart from say two years when I was about five or six, something like that.

Dunn: And who were your heroes? You must have had heroes when you were at school. Who were they?

Gower: Graeme Pollock was the biggest hero I had. Him and Garfield

Sobers were the two. I saw Pollock play at Trent Bridge in the Test match when I was eight and he made a hundred. Now at eight you don't remember too much of these things, just one or two sort of imprints at the back of my mind that I can just recall. When I was seventeen I went to South Africa on a schools trip, and the one day's first-class cricket we saw that time was in Eastern Province, at Port Elizabeth, and he made another hundred. I met him finally this year for the first time. He was over in this country on business, and we managed to get him up to Newcastle to play a couple of games against a combined Durham and Northumberland side, and he made another hundred there, so he hasn't done badly.

Dunn: Great, yes. Illingworth was a great help to you, wasn't he?

Gower: Well yes, when I joined the club next year he was captain, and he and people like Jack Birkenshaw and Mick Norman, what I call the old stalwarts of the club, were all good to me and I learned a lot very quickly those first two years really.

Dunn: Though he thought you were too scruffy, I gather?

Gower: Well, Raymond's quite proud about the way he's dressed, and I suppose my university influences jeans and T shirts, and there were one or two unfortunate incidents. We managed to survive. I did once arrive at Trent Bridge with one black shoe, one brown shoe! I only noticed that the moment I walked into the ground, and he noticed it thirty seconds later.

Dunn: But you retaliated by coming down to breakfast in a dinner jacket!

Gower: Well, we tried that the next time he mentioned the standards of dress. Smart casual is the order of the day in county cricket nowadays – you know, some people interpret that differently. I decided that for Taunton, which was the first away game that year, breakfast would be dinner suit or dinner jacket and bow-tie.

Dunn: And he said?

Gower: He said, 'Have you only just come in?'

Dunn: What's been the sweetest moment so far of your career?

Gower: I think the most satisfying would have been in Jamaica on the West Indies tour, 154 not out against them.

Dunn: Lovely. Well, you've got a tour coming up, of course, New Zealand, Pakistan this winter. When do you go?

Gower: We go just after Christmas. We leave on 29 December, and we stop off two or three days in Fiji. I think it is the first time an England side has been there for about fifty years, and we have to play two one-day games against them.

Dunn: Are you looking forward to the tour?

Gower: Yes, I always do, I think touring's one of the fun parts of cricket. I enjoy the travel, I enjoy being in different places. And you think of the number of people who never get on a tour. If you are there, you've got to enjoy it.

Dunn: And if the chance to become England's captain does arise, you'll be extremely happy?

Gower: Yes, I'd be proud.

*   *   *

AUTUMN CRICKET

The legendary Lord Dunsany, the 18th Baron to boot; to call him names, Edward John Moreton Drax Plunkett, who in his time (1878– 1957) was a big-game hunter, a chess champion, and a prolific poet who scratched out his verses with a quill pen. He was once described as 'the worst-dressed man in Ireland', which has absolutely nothing to do with this charming fantasy which should strike a recapitulatory chord in the soul of every lover of cricket.

Autumn Cricket
Lord Dunsany

Morning Story, Radio 4, December 1986

On one of those short journeys by car that one sometimes takes nowadays I happened to pass after nightfall the once-famous cricket field of Long Barrow. They play there still in the summer, though not so much as they used to do; but this was autumn, when it would be deserted by day, and at night there was nothing there but grey mists that had strayed from a neighbouring stream that winds along under the willows at one end of the ground.

Perhaps it was the contrast between the activity for which that field had been famous and the loneliness of it in that autumn night that made me feel for a moment a sense of desolation. And then my headlights flashed on the face of an old man sitting on a wooden bench by the side of the field and gazing out into the mists, whose shapes floated up from the stream and rose every now and then in little wraiths, as a breeze in the cold night played with them for a while and soon dropped them again.

Somehow this solitary figure there seemed to increase the loneliness. Then just before the light left him, to seep on and illuminate hedges and branches of trees, the old man began to clap. Sitting all alone on that wooden bench, looking over an empty field, he was unmistakably applauding something.

I went on to my destination in the car, and that was all the story I had to tell my friends – a field at night covered with mist, nothing else there, and a man beside it clapping; and not a very likely story either. But I told it, such as it was, to a friend next day who knew Long Barrow, living nearer to it than I do, and this is what he told me.

'Oh, that would have been old Modgers,' he said. 'He used to be groundsman there, but retired on account of age long ago, and has a cottage almost beside it.'

'What was he doing there at that hour?' I asked.

'Well, that's the trouble,' he said. 'It's not good for him at that age to be out in the cold like that, and we can't stop him, unless we have him legally restrained.'

'But surely you can't shut a man up,' I said, 'merely to prevent him from going out in the cold.'

'It's more than that,' he said. 'The old man thinks there's a cricket match going on there every night, and he goes out to look at it.'

'Who does he think is playing?' I asked.

'W. G. Grace,' he replied, 'and Gunn, and a lot of other famous players, all of them men he has seen on that ground, and all of them dead. We are trying to have him certified. And then they'll be able to keep him in at night.'

'Will he like that?' I said rather lamely.

'No,' he said. 'He wants to go and see ghosts playing cricket. But it's the only way to stop him. His wife can't do it.'

'Can you do it on that?' I asked.

'His doctor says so,' said Meadly. That was my friend's name. 'He says he has given him very detailed accounts of the games that he watches, even to the score of each ghost.'

So I imagined that I was never likely to see any more of old Modgers.

And then one day only a week or so later, when autumn was a little colder and mistier, I was passing that way after nightfall again, and there was the same old man sitting on his old wooden bench that was still by the side of the ground, and gazing steadily, just as he had before, at the wisps of mist that breezes lifted over the rest and let fall again into the greyness that went all the way to the stream. So they had not certified the old man, and he was still out there of a night in the cold.

Next day I decided to go to my friend Meadly's house to ask him to tell me more of the story, the beginnings of which he had told me. I rang his bell and he came to the door himself, and I apologised for disturbing him, and told him that old Modgers was still there at night, just as before.

'Come in,' he said cheerily, 'and have some tea, and I'll tell you about him.'

Well, I went into his smoking-room with him and sat down in a comfortable chair, and he said: 'The trouble was that one doctor by himself cannot certify a man. It takes two. That is the law. And the old fellow found out that he was going to be certified, and when the second doctor turned up Modgers wouldn't say a word about ghosts. So, in spite of the evidence of his own doctor, we have been unable to get him into an asylum.'

'Well, I suppose we'd all try to escape that if we could,' I said.

'It isn't the asylum that he jibs at,' said Meadly, 'but he won't leave his ghosts. You see, he's somewhere in his late eighties, and kept that ground for nearly fifty years and played on it before that; and to give up cricket is to him what giving up much more important things would be to others, and he thinks he's still watching it. Of course, if we could prove that, we could get him certified. But we can't. His doctor had the whole story from him; but that is not enough. We've asked his wife to wrap him up as much as possible. And she does that, but we can't stop him.'

'Perhaps it would be possible to reason with him,' I said, as tea was brought in by a maid.

'I don't think so,' he said.

'I'd like to try,' I told him. 'He can't want to be frozen to death.'

'Men don't like to be killed by any of their follies,' said Meadly, 'but they don't like to give them up. And I suppose more good advice is wasted on asking them if they wouldn't like to do so than on anything in the world.'

'Still, I'd like to try,' I said.

And so I added myself to the number of those who ask men to give up the harmful things they like most in life, one in every hundred thousand of whom succeed. So why shouldn't I? I went over by bus next night to Long Barrow an hour or two after sunset and walked alone to the cricket-ground. And sure enough he was on his usual bench, looking out over the famous ground at the first thin wisps of mist that were coming up from the stream and nearing the lonely pitch.

I went up to the wooden bench and sat down beside him. He hastily looked all round, evidently to satisfy himself that two men were not within hearing, and not till he had thoroughly scrutinised the misty darkness did he say anything to me. But then he spoke.

'They are just coming in to bat,' he said. 'That's Gunn, and that's W.G.'

'So I see,' I replied.

'You know them, then?' he asked.

'By sight,' I said.

'They often play here,' he told me.

'Do you watch them often?' I asked.

'Whenever they play,' he said.

'Is it a good thing to be out so late with all this mist rising?' I asked him.

'They never play by day,' he said.

'But are you sure you are warm enough?' I asked.

'I wrap up well,' he said. 'And I never stay more than two hours, unless it's a very exciting game. And I go to bed as soon as I get home.'

He stopped to clap then, gazing over the ground towards the approaching mist. And I thought over what he had said, and it seemed to me that if he was really well wrapped up under the good greatcoat that he wore, and if he did not stay more than two hours, it might not be so serious as Meadly and others feared, at any rate not till the winter.

And so I told Meadly next day. I sat there beside the old fellow for nearly half an hour and heard an excellent summary of a very exciting game, something I suppose that had remained in his memory, which was still fresh and vivid whatever had happened to the rest of his mind, perhaps over-weighted and upset by the sheer power of that part of the brain that stores and preserves past days. It was really a very exciting match. I remember it yet. W. G. won, though that proves nothing, because he nearly always did.

I saw Modgers home hale and hearty, and I went to Meadly next day and urged him to leave the old man alone, at least till winter came, and told him that I felt sure he would be all right. And I think I persuaded Meadly. But long before winter was here the old man died.

What happened, as we afterwards heard from his wife, was, only a fortnight later, being a bit older than Meadly had thought, he reached his ninetieth birthday. And old Mrs Modgers told us that on that very evening, while they were having a bit of a supper and a glass of wine with which to celebrate the occasion, the mist having risen as it always did in the autumn, but no higher than one of their windows, old Modgers had glanced out of the window and suddenly said they had made him an honorary member, an honorary member of the ghosts who used to play at Long Barrow, because he was ninety. And Modgers had said that this was a great honour, because he was the only living man that had been invited to play at night on that ground. And they were going to play that night, Modgers had said; and the Doctor himself, that is Dr Grace, had invited Modgers to play for him. So Modgers had gone; she couldn't stop him. And this time he wouldn't even dress up warm.

'Well,' she said, 'he went out there with his bat, for he had an old bat that he still kept in a cupboard, and he said he wouldn't want pads, because the ball they were using wasn't as hard as all that, and he went out to the pitch and bent down like as if he was batting, and began hitting about.'

'But surely,' Meadly said to her, 'he didn't run.'

'He seemed to be hitting boundaries,' said Mrs Modgers. 'I stayed and watched the whole time, but he wouldn't allow me to bring him home. He seemed to be hitting boundaries, and so did the gentleman opposite to him, whoever that may have been, or perhaps I should say *whatever,* seeing they was all ghosts, but for him. But after he had hit about twenty of them he seemed to get tired and not to be able to hit so far, and then he had to run. I couldn't stop him. And after a while he took off his hat two or three times and looked round about him, seemingly very pleased. And I think he had got his century.

'And that was when it happened. Of course a man of his age couldn't run like he did, and he dropped dead. I could do nothing.'

We both made those vain attempts that people sometimes make with words, trying to comfort Mrs Modgers. But, though we knew we could bring her no comfort whatever, we both of us saw a gleam on her face that seemed, faint though it was, to shine from a hidden smile, as she said, 'They were never able to shut him up in no asylum. And he'll be able to play at Long Barrow now with Doctor Grace and Mr Gunn whenever he likes.'

*　　　*　　　*

INDEX

Italic figures refer to illustrations

Acknowledgements

Pictures
Page 65 (top left), 66 (bottom), 68 (bottom), 69 (bottom), 70 (bottom),
71 (bottom), 137 (top), 138 (bottom), 140 (bottom) and 143 (bottom left)
THE KEYSTONE COLLECTION; Pages 65 (top right & bottom), 66 (top), 67
(top & bottom), 72, 140 (top), 143 (bottom right) and 144 (bottom) BBC
HULTON PICTURE LIBRARY; Pages 68 (top), 69 (top), 70 (top), 140 (centre)
and 144 (top) POPPERFOTO; Page 71 (top) BBC (Geoff Sherlock); Page 137
(bottom) GUBBY ALLEN; Page 138 (top) from 'Women's Test Cricket The
Golden Triangle 1934–84' by Joan L. Hawes; Page 139 (top & bottom)
PATRICK EAGAR; Page 141 (top & bottom) ALLSPORT PHOTOGRAPHIC (Adrian
Murrell); Page 143 (top) ALLSPORT PHOTOGRAPHIC; and page 142 BOB
THOMAS SPORTS PHOTOGRAPHY.

Text
The author and publishers would like to thank the contributors for
permission to reproduce their material. They have endeavoured to trace
all copyright holders but if they have unwittingly infringed copyright, they
apologise and would be pleased to hear from copyright holders.